Kuki Gallmann

AFRICAN NIGHTS

VIKING

VIKING

Published by the Penguin Group
Penguin Books Ltd, 27 Wrights Lane, London w8 5TZ, England
Penguin Books USA Inc., 375 Hudson Street, New York, New York 10014, USA
Penguin Books Australia Ltd, Ringwood, Victoria, Australia
Penguin Books Canada Ltd, 10 Alcorn Avenue, Toronto, Ontario, Canada M4V 3B2
Penguin Books (NZ) Ltd, 182–190 Wairau Road, Auckland 10, New Zealand

Penguin Books Ltd, Registered Offices: Harmondsworth, Middlesex, England

First published 1994
1 3 5 7 9 10 8 6 4 2
First edition

Filmset by Datix International Limited, Bungay, Suffolk
Printed in England by Clays Ltd, St Ives plc
Set in 12½/15½ pt Monophoto Bembo

A CIP catalogue record for this book is available from the British Library

ISBN 0–670–85611–8

The Gallmann Memorial Foundation,
PO Box 45593, Nairobi, Kenya

For Sveva, with my love for ever

Listen attentively, and above all remember that true tales are meant to be transmitted; to keep them to oneself is to betray them.

Baal–Schem–Tov (Israel ben Eliezer)

CONTENTS

PREFACE

When I sit with my daughter by a campfire, or in front of the fireplace at Kuti, and the peculiar silence of the African night is full of the voices of a million crickets, and interrupted by a far-away hyena, by a lion's roar or by our dogs barking suddenly at shadows of elephants, I remember the adventures of the past, the people I have known, the men we have lost, and I tell her their stories.

I was born in Italy and from my earliest childhood I dreamed of Africa. After my recovery from a tragic accident which left me crippled, I went to live in Kenya with my second husband, Paolo, his two daughters and the son of my early marriage, Emanuele, then six years old. We bought a house in Nairobi, in an area called Gigiri, and spent much time exploring the country, and particularly the coast, where we used to spend most of the holidays. After many adventures we acquired Ol Ari Nyiro, a vast ranch on the Laikipia plateau, overlooking the Great Rift Valley, which became our home.

The ranch was magnificent and abounded with wildlife. We managed it to keep a balance between agriculture and livestock and the conservation of the environment, and those were happy, unforgettable days. We learned to know Africa, to love its people and to protect its wild animals and plants.

In 1980 Paolo was killed in a car accident a few months before the birth of our child, while he was bringing me her crib, a wooden boat made out of a tree trunk by fishermen at the coast. Sveva was born beautiful and the image of her father. I chose to remain in Laikipia. Here Emanuele, who was now fourteen, who since his early childhood had shown an unusual intelligence and a maturity beyond his years, and who had always been interested in animals, developed a deep passion for snakes.

At seventeen Emanuele was killed by one of his vipers while extracting venom for the manufacture of anti-poison vaccine. He died in my arms in a few minutes. I buried him next to Paolo, at the bottom of my garden at Kuti, and planted on each grave a thorn tree. As a mother I felt that nothing could ever again heal my wounds, but although it deeply affected me, Emanuele's death did not alter my love for the country of my choice. On the contrary, it strengthened my resolve to become even more actively involved in its preservation.

In memory of Paolo and of Emanuele I founded The Gallmann Memorial Foundation, which aims to create at Ol Ari Nyiro an example of the harmonious coexistence of man with the wild, through studying new ways of protecting nature through utilization. The symbol of the Foundation is the two trees which grow on the graves.

I have always loved books and am fascinated by the music of words. Eventually I wrote the story of my life, which I called *I Dreamed of Africa.*

There is too much in a life to be able to concentrate it just in one book. It is too early to write a continuation of my autobiography, as the significance of events only becomes clear with the perspective that time can give memories. This is a collection of true episodes, some of which developed at the same time as my story, and some which had not yet occurred. They are linked by my love of Africa and its mysterious creatures, by my wonder at its beauty and pervasive magic, and by my nostalgia for the past.

Kuki Gallmann,
Laikipia, March 1994

ACKNOWLEDGEMENTS

A number of friends have encouraged and advised me during the writing of this book. I am particularly indebted to:

Gilfrid Powys, for his total confidence in me; Chris Thouless, for his witty criticism and intelligent humour; Adrian House, for calling me a story-teller; Toby Eady, for his professional and brotherly support; John and Buffy Sacher, for the generosity with which they made me welcome again and again in their home in London; my Kenyan friends; the scores of people who wrote just to let me know that my earlier book had helped their own life in some way, and who asked me to continue to write.

And, as ever, to Paolo and Emanuele, whose memory infuses my life with light and a sense of purpose.

And to my daughter Sveva, for being here.

LIST OF ILLUSTRATIONS

All photographs by the author except where indicated

Colour

1. The house and garden at Kuti
2. Kuki and Sveva   (Photo: Mark Bader)
3. Emanuele and a pet young agama
4. Tigger
5. Ol Ari Nyiro: cheetah at Nagiri dam   (Photo: Lissa Ruben)
6. The Pokot women come to Kuti   (Photo: John Sacher)
7 & 8.   A hoopoe flew on to Paolo's head   (Photo: Fabio Sole)
9. Ben, Paolo and the Bullshark of Vuma   (Photo: Franco Ongaro)
10. Sveva and Meave at Ol Ari Nyiro Springs
11. Elephant seen from the treetop below Paolo's dam
12. Elephants drinking at a dam   (Photo: John Sacher)
13. Ekiru Mirimuk guarding the hills   (Photo: Lissa Ruben)
14. Kuki and baby rhino   (Photo: Yann Arthur-Bertrand)
15. Lake Turkana

16. The pool at Maji ya Nyoka   (Photo: Lissa Ruben)
17. Kuki and camel
18. Sveva riding camels in the Amaya Valley
19. Osman with the female camel and baby
20. Borau tells his adventure
21. Emanuele in the snake pit at Kuti

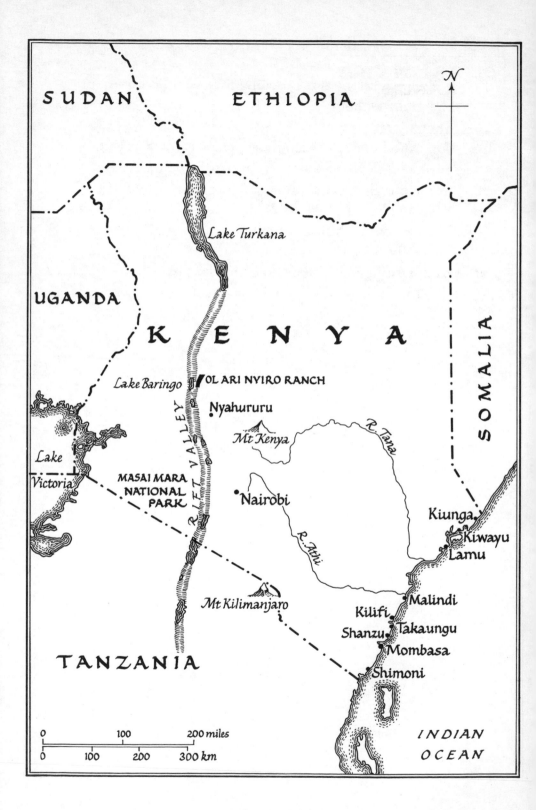

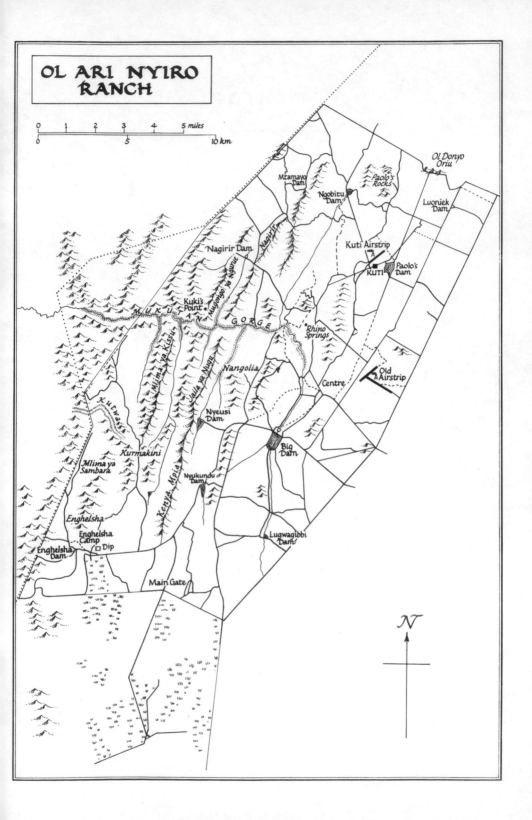

OL ARI NYIRO RANCH

0 1 2 3 4 5 miles
0   5   10 km

Mtamayo Dam

Ngobitu Dam

Paolo's Rocks

Ol Donyo Oriu

Luoniek Dam

Nagirir Dam

Kuti Airstrip

KUTI

Paolo's Dam

Kuki's Point

Mugongo ya Ngurue

Nagirir

MUKUTAN GORGE

Mlima ya Kisiru

Rhino Springs

Nangolia

Jaha ya Nuru

Nyeusi Dam

Centre

Old Airstrip

Kutwa

Kurmakini

Big Dam

Mlima ya Sambara

Nyukundu Dam

Kenya Mpia

Enghelsha

Enghelsha Camp

Dip

Lugwagibbi Dam

Enghelsha Dam

Main Gate

N

I

FULL-MOON ISLAND

What if this present were the world's last night?
John Donne, *Holy Sonnets*, xiii

When we went to live in Africa, we spent our first Christmas holiday at the coast. Although the magnificent beaches and pure coral reef were already beginning to attract the attention of international tourism, it was early days. The coastline of Kenya was largely still the kingdom of seagulls and turtles, of wooden dhows built from hollow tree trunks, of Giriama and Swahili fishermen singing to the tides a song of waves and hope of fish.

A few local pockets of quiet middle-aged people of European origin were attached to coastal villages. Their favourite spots were Malindi, Kilifi, Vipingo, Shanzu and Shimoni.

They were an unusual community of retired residents, mostly former farmers, who had sold their up-country properties, at the foot of Mount Kenya, in the dry windswept Highlands, or in the green tea and coffee districts of Kericho and Thika. Undisturbed and undisturbing, comforted by an assortment of dogs and generous sundowners, they now spent their sunset days in the breezy shade of their spacious verandahs. Their new homes, built mostly of white-washed coral blocks, with tall roofs of thatched palm leaves, were immersed in intricate gardens of bougainvilleas and mango trees and graced by a constant view of the shimmering reef.

They owned boats of various descriptions, grand ocean cruisers, or modest homemade catamarans, which they tended meticulously, since they all shared a consuming passion for deep sea fishing, or sailing, or both.

The sea had always held a peculiar attraction for Paolo, who loved to explore it, and before we found our own promised land we spent much time there. For people who lived alone in the silence of their memories, and who could understandably have been diffident of strangers, the Kenya coast community were sociable, and made us instantly welcome. Perhaps the fact that we were young, enchanted with the ocean as they were, exotic, carefree and in love, with charming, sunny children, and all the time in the world, triggered their curiosity and an unexpressed nostalgia for days gone by. They offered us, with total generosity, the hospitality of their homes, boats and drinks cabinets, and the friendship of their pets.

With unexpected inventiveness, they devised occasional entertainments to interrupt the monotony of their unbroken days. One night in Shimoni, just before the New Year, they asked us, and my mother who had come to visit us in Africa for the first time, to a full-moon picnic dinner out in the ocean, on an island which only emerged with the low tide.

'Shall we go?' Paolo asked, a blue glint in his eyes. 'The night is going to be clear, a fantastic light.'

A teasing note: 'Yet, it is rather far. It might be wet . . . late for the children and your mother. We'll have to use a compass to find the way. It sounds mad.'

It did. And irresistible.

'*Andiamo,*' I said. Italian was all I could then speak.

We assembled at dusk on the shore below one of the houses. Cool boxes and baskets crowded together, packed with food which revealed the origin of their owners: pickled herrings in dill and deadly schnapps for the Scandinavian; smoked salmon sandwiches, scotch eggs, blue cheese and beer for the English; white cheese, olives and divine ouzo for the few Greek; and for us, of course, pizzas, salame, provolone and flasks of red Chianti and chilled white Fol. We also had the large classic panettone which is the taste of any Italian Christmas, and which my mother, now slightly bewildered by this adventure, had heroically carried all the way from Venice.

Only in groups made up predominantly of British people can a 'quiet excitement' prevail: active, efficient, aiming at a goal. In this atmosphere the boats were loaded, darkness fell, and we went.

The humid warmth of a salty breeze beaded our faces, and the black oily surface of the ocean opened smoothly to our bows, and closed in a wake of glimmering foam. The plankton shone phosphorescent like submerged galaxies, drawing patterns on the disturbed surface. The engines droned on. Emanuele, a little boy of six, came to rest close to me, and the night was reflected in his large dark eyes, which absorbed everything. Someone sang a slow song which blended with the talking voices, and the engine noise, and the smell of seaweed.

For hours we went far into the blackness. Then, at a point in the ocean which seemed identical to any other, the leading boat came to a sudden halt, its engine slowed to a murmur. We all grew silent, and watched in bated expectation while the horizon glowed lighter and the ink of the night became a blue velvet drape on which stars gradually paled like dying candles. As the breeze seemed to grow into a strange wind, and the current lapping the sides of the boat to be sucked away faster and faster, the largest white moon began to rise, sailing over the horizon.

By and by, massive and silent, the mystery island began to appear in front of our eyes. First the coral rocks emerged, like the crested back of a sleeping sea monster; then a startlingly white, smooth beach of opal began to materialize, matching the cold moon. Dinghies were lowered from all the boats, and efficiently loaded with the food baskets, barbecues and crates of bottles. People started eagerly rowing ashore.

I was allotted a tiny yellow rubber dinghy, wet and slippery, in which I sat at the oars, with Emanuele, a case of beer and a cluster of bananas. I started rowing, but had not appreciated the speed of the current. The wind blew stronger. Twenty minutes went by, and I did not seem to have made any progress. I was drenched and cold. Our friends seemed far away, the shore unattainable, and the wind did not carry my voice.

Paolo finally came to my rescue, laughing. In no time I was ashore on the firm, cool sand, safe in his arms, drinking a glass of wine.

People were scattered in small groups, divided or united by their age, taste, spirit, hunger or thirst. The charcoal was lit with some difficulty, helped by the blue flame of paraffin, which the wind soon transmuted into a glowing orange warmth on the wrought iron barbecue. The smell of grilling marinated chicken, fizzling sausages and garlic bread came in whiffs of fragrant smoke billowing on the wind.

The chilled oily schnapps, drunk enthusiastically in tiny glasses, raised the spirits high in minutes, chasing away the shivers, while the jolly noise of popping corks filled the night.

A group of children sang with a guitar. Others ran along the beach, pursuing crabs. Emanuele went alone with his torch, looking for imprudent cowries left out on the shore by the receding tide. Even my mother seemed to have found someone with whom to talk.

Mellowed and content, I unrolled a straw mat and sat on it thinking my thoughts, wrapped in a *kanga*, watching Paolo turning the grilled meat with hungry dexterity, opening bottles, chatting away in English, totally integrated.

Hours went by, and with time we grew silent. A subtle muting again, a shudder in the breeze. The tide was coming back. Slowly at first, then faster and faster, the waves began to reclaim the sand, inch by inch. And with the advancing water, changed our mood.

Out on the invisible full-moon island in the middle of the Indian Ocean everything seemed possible. Was the rest of the world still there?

Italy, recently left, now seemed so far.

Mad thoughts of returning to find no Shimoni, no more shores anywhere on which to land, just a limitless ocean where tongues of beach like this one appeared only for a few hours with the moon. Forever vagabonds on the wild seas like the Flying Dutchman.

'*Passa la nave mia con vele nere . . .* '★

Time to go back. A sudden forewarning, a void, a fear.

I looked for Emanuele. He was running after his dreams in the wind along the shore, minute and unreachable as an elf in a fairy tale, and his hair had the colour of the waning moon. With a squeeze in my chest I called him, and my voice came back to me in the night, like a lost seagull's.

Then Paolo was with him. They were running together, and they were holding hands.

★ 'There goes my vessel with the black sails.'

2

EMANUELE'S CHAMELEONS

On a souvent besoin d'un plus petit que soi★
Jean de La Fontaine, *Fables*, II. 11
'Le Lion et le Rat'

'I remember him well,' said the pretty young woman I had just met, looking at me with a shy smile. 'We were in the same class at school, when we were children. He was kind, quiet and different. I was sad when he died.'

Her eyes in the darkness seemed misty – or was it a candle-light illusion? 'He always kept chameleons in his desk.'

'Pep, look what I found!' A greyish miniature dragon clung tenaciously to his straight blond hair. I gasped. It was an ugly thing, with rough skin covered in round dry blisters, three crested protuberances on its nose, curiously like a rhino, and a large toothless mouth, frog-like and quite repulsive. With consummate gentleness Emanuele disentangled the creature, and held it out for me to see.

It was a March afternoon in Nairobi, after one of the first sudden showers of the long rains, which leave an intense smell of wet soil and fresh hay and are followed by a violent sun that instantly dries the drops trapped in the grass. Emanuele looked at me with his deep eyes of brown velvet, shadowed by unknown melancholies older than his years.

'It is a Jackson's chameleon, Pep,' he said proudly. 'I found it in the bamboos.' He contemplated it admiringly.

★ 'One often needs someone smaller than oneself.'

'Don't you think it looks like a *Triceratops*? Can I keep it, please? His name is King Alfred.'

King Alfred was the British king who fought against the Danes. In Emanuele's history book they wore the horned helmets of the legendary Vikings. I suppose that first chameleon owed his regal name to this association.

I nodded weakly. A quick glint of triumph lit his eyes.

So began Emanuele's love of reptiles, his passion for chameleons, and an extraordinary capacity for finding them wherever he went. He had been born a collector. As a small child he had collected minerals, shells and small model animals. Later, snakes would take over as his abiding passion. When chameleons became the first reptiles he officially owned, I did not know that we had entered a new era, and that there would be no going back. He was six. In a few years snakes would lead him inexorably to his destiny.

Soon we all liked King Alfred.

He did indeed look like a gigantic herbivorous dinosaur which had existed in the Cretaceous period, as I learnt from one of Emanuele's books which I went to check for reference. In fact, dinosaurs had entered our household years earlier, when my father, during his peregrinations, had discovered a sensational deposit of their bones on a fossil river bed in the Ténéré desert. A black and white photograph of Emanuele aged four, reaching out to the tall skeleton of a monstrous *Diplodocus*, to impress the reader with its size in relation to our miserable human proportions, appeared in a book in which my father wrote his adventure.

Unlike me, Emanuele knew all about dinosaurs, their looks, names and habits, and undoubtedly there was a very strong similarity between the original *Triceratops* and its enigmatic descendant which had come to live with us. A chameleon is a creature of marked individuality, and I could easily see how a curious and intelligent boy, fascinated by animals, could be mesmerized by this deliberate and friendly little monster.

During the day, King Alfred lived in a box full of leaves and small branches. Emanuele fed him with insects which he captured at school, whenever he had a free moment, and kept in an old jam jar. Often, however, he smuggled the chameleon to school in a small perforated cardboard box, and at break time would let him climb on the low shrubs in the school yard, and observe, enraptured, the antics of his hunt.

King Alfred was a few inches long. His legs ended in hands shaped like pincers, with strong fingers sprouting at opposite angles to allow a sturdy hold on the flimsiest of stems and shoots. His curly and prehensile tail could twist quickly around the most minute asperities of leaves and twigs, with a precarious sense of balance, like a monkey diving from the highest trees in the forest.

His most striking feature, however, was his eyes, stereoscopic instruments independently rotating to focus, through the holes of the irises, along a narrow field of vision that ensured the infallible aim of the spring of his viscous tongue.

An unsuspecting grasshopper swayed on a blade of grass; his tongue would dart out faster than our sudden repugnance, which lingered well after the insect had disappeared into the cavernous mouth. We caught our breath in horror.

In time, however, I grew used to this revolting performance and even found a certain fascination in watching its precision, which reminded me of the skill of a cowboy's lasso, or of the cruel, mindless catapult that interrupts the free flight of a bird.

It was the strangest thing of all to watch the colours vary in King Alfred's grainy skin. Brown in the sun, he changed to unexpected shades of emerald green in the shade. On my yellow bedspread one day, he turned a bright lemon hue in less than a minute, as if invisible brush strokes had gradually repainted him in front of my eyes.

His presence disrupted somehow the household's activities, because servants refused to enter the room where they thought he might be. Our cook Gathimu and the house servant Bitu always avoided the study in which Emanuele's new friend wandered about freely, presiding over his homework in the afternoons, perched on books, scanning the ceiling for flies and mosquitoes, and stalking with silent glee the lazy, sluggish house-insects.

Many legends are linked to the chameleon in Africa, possibly derived from its mysterious mimetism. Africans therefore traditionally dislike them and prefer not to go near them. In the local legends the chameleon plays the part which, in the Bible, is attributed to the snake who tempted Eve in the garden of Eden: a strange conspiracy with the woman like whom it is variable, fluid, constantly changing into a fantasy of rainbows.

This dubious aura of 'untouchability' is what saves chameleons. It allows them to move around with impunity their defenceless prehistoric bodies, whose only natural enemies are snakes and birds of prey, who neither read books nor listen to stories.

King Alfred was the first of many. There followed various Marshall's chameleons, small and dark. A couple of rather fat ones, which were in fact named Fatty I and Fatty II: they did not have the protuberances on their noses and looked, more than anything, like hypocritical frogs. After them we had a Robert the Bruce, a Victor, a Kiwi, a 'Pembe Nussu' (or 'half horn' – it was mutilated), and King Alfred II. There were many more whose names I have forgotten. My son cared for them lovingly, letting them walk in the bamboos and on the gardenia outside my door, which attracted a myriad insects with its rich perfume.

Then there was the time when three chameleons came with us on an expedition to Lake Turkana – still called Lake Rudolph in those days – because Emanuele refused to leave them behind. It was the hot and dry time before the April rains, during the Easter holidays. The journey from Nairobi took two days on the dusty tracks, and it was slowed further by our stops to look after the chameleons. Each time, their box was opened so that they could breathe fresh air, and be sprayed with cool water. They even managed to catch a couple of flies.

Yet the heat of the glove compartment in the Land Rover was extreme, overwhelming.

When, after hours of bumps, in the late afternoon of the second day, the breathtaking expanse of the lake, with its islands and shores of black lava and yellow grasses, appeared below the last bend like a primitive vision, Fatty I was dead.

In the open box littered with dried flies, his elongated body looked weirdly colourless, like the negative image of what it had once been. It had the temporary and precarious quality of frailness which belongs to small archaeological finds, discovered in the secret recesses of broken, desecrated sepulchres, which may disintegrate with the fresh air of day. It would not have surprised me if what was left of Fatty I had suddenly dissolved into pale dust.

This drama shadowed our jolliness. When, miles afterwards, we reached the oasis of Loyangalani, we left the car to have a drink and find relief in the shady breeze of the palm grove. Emanuele did not join us. He went off alone amongst the bristling grasses beside the path leading to the hot thermal springs.

When he came back he did not have the box, and his eyes glinted below the blond fringe. He had let the survivors go free in an environment that could allow their survival.

Somewhere, under a lava stone, rested what remained of Fatty I. We matched Emanuele's sorrow with our silence.

Not so long ago, looking through his old yellowed papers, which have become precious relics to me now, I found a large blue exercise book roughly bound by himself. On the cover, a childish hand had written in red: 'My Chameleons'.

I leafed through it. It was dated July 1975, and it was written in English. Its tidy pages recorded, in his minute neat handwriting, names and dates, families, species, favourite foods and other details of every one of his chameleons; one of the pages was folded, wrinkled up and partly torn in small pieces.

I unravelled it carefully.

The passage was almost unreadable. It ended like this:

. . . Chameleons are extraordinary animals and fascinating hunters. I began to love them in 1972, and still now, in 1975, I love them. My favourites were Fatty I and Fatty II. They were very fast in eating, but slow in all their other movements. Whenever I let them go or whenever they escaped, I always found them again. Fatty I died of heat at Lake Rudolph.

On the word 'died', the pen had faltered.

3

THE BRIGADIER'S CHEETAH

The sleek and shining creatures of the chase
Alfred, Lord Tennyson,
'The Revenge', v, 147

Sometimes in the afternoons of the holidays, when we were in Nairobi, at our house near Rosslynn, Emanuele asked me to go with him to see Tigger: he remembered the night when we had encountered him, and how he had not run away when he saw us.

Tigger was a male cheetah, a few years old, who lived on the coffee farm of one of our neighbours, a retired army Brigadier.

We used to jump into the car, and set off, leaving the tarmac road for a red murram track winding through coffee bushes. Soon the usual scene would appear. Along the slope they walked slowly, among the tall dry grasses, their patient black dogs following quietly, wagging their tails in rhythm. A girl pushed a pram from which peered the freckled faces of two children. Next, tall and slightly bent, leaning on a golf club, came the Brigadier, with his wife, and the cheetah.

The cheetah moved lightly, the fluffy tip of his tail barely brushing the ground. His easy gait had the grace of a dance rhythmed to the silent beat of distant drums. A leash circled his chest. He advanced sure and languid, his small head buried between powerful shoulders, his one eye yellow and alert, its colour matching his coat maculated with regular black spots. Emanuele ran out to hug him, and the rough tongue licked friendly his young neck and cheeks. The eye closed in pleasure, and the cheetah purred like a large happy cat.

This was the evening walk, amongst the coffee bushes along the slopes behind the house, the same now for years. Ever since he had been found, with two other cubs, after their mother had been killed during a long chase in the savannah, he had been kept and cared for, chosen from among the litter because of a congenital eye defect that would never allow him to hunt alone and to be independent like his brothers.

When they called him 'Tigger' he was just a kitten, as soft as a real toy and defenceless as any rejected puppy. They called him Tigger, a fierce name, but he was gentle. Only when wild rabbits darted from their holes in the red earth to disappear in mad leaps through the undergrowth, did his young muscles tense, and he would coil in the ancestral instinct, ready to spring after a running prey.

For play companions Tigger had three Labrador puppies, recently born in their mother's basket behind the outside staircase, which the Golden Shower covered with cascades of orange blossoms, sheltering it like a real lair in the forest. The playful fights with the puppies on the lawn, the habit of sharing bones, the sudden frantic sprints and the deep sleeps of abandon, tummies up on the grass, and eyes closed against the implacable glare of the Equator's sun, made them brothers and inseparable. He was never alone, and who knows if in the flat compact head dreams ever drifted of runs over plains in the short red sunsets, when the Highlands plains are alive with herds of gazelle, and predators emerge from the shadows of the day with silent steps, to sniff the scent of the preys of the night.

Often, at a sudden movement, he lifted his head. His round black nostrils vibrated sensitively to imperceptible scents, and the ears tensed to the inaudible shuffle of near, secret lives. The amber-and-honey eye scrutinized the horizon like an eye-glass: even the faintest shiver in the savannah grass did not escape his gaze. A black line circled his eye sockets like a mask and defined his round features, dividing them with two black tears which slid down to the corners of his mouth. In his black war paint his face looked sad.

He played with the dogs, more dog than cat, lacking retractable claws; he looked like a large greyhound, to which a feline head had been attached. His fine legs were far slenderer than the powerful, stocky ones of a lion; his paws far slighter than the rounded catty ones of a leopard. He moved lightly, with a lazy elegance born of the assurance of being safe.

His mother had given birth to her cubs alone, in the shade of the large acacia, amongst the low shrubs which protected her from the eyes of her natural enemies, the hyena and the wild dogs. Alone she had brought them up, leaving them for entire days while she stalked the plains, alert and sinewy, her graceful tail flowing like a mane in the winds of adventure.

They had soon learned to be independent, helped by nature which had given them a crest of odd long hairs on the top of their heads, white and straight to match the long highland grasses bleached by the African sun. This allowed them to hide, camouflaged even amongst the driest of sticks and thorns, until their mother returned at dusk, to feed them with swollen breasts, the smell of a Thomson's gazelle's blood still in her breath.

But one night she did not come back, and the hunter found them, hungry and torpid next day, huddled together for comfort in the shade of the acacia tree.

He grew with the puppies and he looked funny and out of place among the black coats; his white tuft stood out pathetically on the green lawn, so different from the silvery waves of the savannah grass stirred by sudden winds. He grew swiftly, unaware of his great strength and grace, until he was

1. Emanuele and Kaa

4. Kilifi: Emanuele

5. Shimoni: Paolo and Emanuele shared a deep passion for fishing

6. Emanuele loved the sea and sailing

7. An adventurous childhood: Charlie Mason and Emanuele riding
bareback in Ngobithu's dam

8. Emanuele and Charlie playing with a young python

9. Paolo spraying the roof infested by caterpillars

10. Building a stone bed: Kuki with Lwokwolognei and Langat

finally an adult: and in the nights of March Tigger suddenly felt the call of his race, even though the farm where he lived was on the edge of the city, and the noise of passing cars and lorries filtered through the narrow cluster of forest like an intrusion into his loneliness.

A tame female cheetah lived not far away, in a garden protected by bougainvillea, dogs and high hibiscus hedges.

One night we came back late from a party, and, at the corner of our road, amongst sisal and giant poinsettias, Emanuele's sharp eyes distinguished a motionless shape, outlined by the full moonlight in all its wild beauty.

He sat perfectly still, like a statue of a sphinx, under the pepper tree, next to the sign board inscribed with our name. His neck was tense, his nostrils flared to sense the breeze. A low, breathy noise, a deep intermittent growl, perhaps a mating call, came from his splendid throat.

The dogs in the neighbourhood began to bark furiously from all the gardens, howling their unrest to the moon. Neither this commotion nor our approaching car seemed to disturb him.

'Tigger,' whispered Emanuele softly from the car window.

Tigger turned his head slowly, to look straight at us, fearless, remote, surrounded by his mystery.

A moment, and he was gone, swallowed by the darkness.

It was after then, I imagine, that the legend of the leopard of Rosslyn was born. Someone else saw him, and gave out an imprecise description. Everybody locked in their dogs at night for a time, as the leopard's predilection for eating dogs is well known.

Not us. We knew it was simply Tigger who wandered for miles and miles, from his safe dog's bed and warm blanket to answer the call of his dormant, never fulfilled instinct. We had phoned the Brigadier, and he saw that the gate was still locked but the basket was empty in the moonlit night. Even if there was no need, as a cheetah can jump high and swift, he left the door of the enclosure open.

Next morning Tigger was there, impassive and tame, as if nothing had happened, to play with the dogs, and to wait for the leash and his evening walk among the coffee bushes: like in an old print, sunlit from the back.

Some time later, to everyone's wonder, our neighbour's female cheetah gave birth.

One of the cubs had an inherited eye defect, and we all knew what had happened.

4

A MAASAI WOMAN

In the face of some Masai matriarchs could be read the tale of a people whose iron code of tradition makes them unique among the earth's beings.

Robert Vavra, *A Tent with a View*

The woman who came through the camp was lean and tall. She could have been of any age between eighteen and thirty. She marched straight towards me in the yellow August dawn, while I stretched to chase away the shadows of sleep, shivering in the early-morning air of the coldest month of the year on the Kenya Highlands. It was 1973, when hunting was still allowed in Kenya.

She greeted me in Swahili and in a high clear voice, without any shyness, she asked me immediately for salt.

'*Chumvi. Mimi nataka chumvi.*' She smiled with even, well-spaced teeth.

All creatures in the Highlands need salt to supplement their diet. Rock salt mixed with the soil creates a salt lick irresistible to elephant, rhino, antelope and buffalo. They walk long miles at dusk, drawn by its subtle scent, imperceptible to human nostril. But before leaving the shelter of the shrubs around the area of the salt-lick, which generations of converging animals' hooves have made barren of vegetation, they pause and sniff the air with quivering muzzles, with tentative trunks, to detect any smell of danger in the wind. Reassured, they move on, head down, eager to lick the salt trapped in the earth.

Chumvi. A handful of the precious salt is a treat that few humans, even, can resist in wild Africa.

I smiled up at her, and nodded. She came close on elegant legs, and sat in the dust next to me.

We had camped in the late afternoon, not far from a *manyatta* in the area of Narok, one of the main centres of the proud Maasai tribe. It then consisted of a couple of petrol stations, a general store kept, like most other stores, by Indian merchants, and a few primitive *dukas*, shops where one can find a bit of everything, from tea to blankets, from dark sugar-cane to snuff, from tinned beans to tablets to fight – often in vain – the endemic malaria.

We had chosen a spot in the shade of some yellow fever trees, and at nightfall had lit a fire of sticks and dry branches. There we had barbecued, on some rudimentary iron wire, the tender fillet of a Thomson's gazelle that had not been fast enough.

The *manyatta* was a large one, composed, like all others, of longish low huts rounded like loaves. Made from a mixture of mud and dung plastered on a frame of curved sticks, they reminded me of dried-out chrysalises. The huts were surrounded by a thick barricade of acacia and 'wait-a-bit' thorn branches, arranged so that the spikes were impenetrable by animal or man.

Cattle are the wealth that the God Ngai – the sky in Maasai – had bestowed for ever on the Maasai race, and it was within this enclosure that their livestock spent the night, each animal packed close to the other, sheltered from predators and cattle rustlers.

The woman was dressed in goatskins, reddened with fat and ochre. From her right ear, stretched down to her shoulder, hung a tin ornament polished like silver and shaped like an arrow. Her left ear was studded with an old beer bottle top, shiny as a new coin.

Her right leg, from ankle to knee, was encased in a spiral-
ling brass bracelet, so tight that it scarcely allowed any space
for her slim bird-like leg. This was so skeletal that it reminded
me of the ancient Roman shinbones I had once found as a
child in a newly ploughed field I was exploring with my
father in the countryside around Quarto d'Altino. How far
from Africa my childhood seemed, yet how close.

Her ornaments showed that this woman was married.
Innumerable rows of small coloured beads swayed gently
from her neck, on her forehead, and around her stunning
black eyes, like a dancing mask. They were threaded with
infinite patience, extravagant skill and a symmetrical elegance
that no mirror had suggested. They framed her tilted eyes,
around which countless flies, motionless and undisturbed,
formed dainty patterns like *points d'esprit* on the lacy veil of
an Edwardian bonnet.

I poured the salt straight from the plastic bag on to her
pink palm, proffered as a cup held between her slender black
fingers. She licked it laughing, greedily, like the most sought
after delicacy. Only when she had finished, and I had put the
remainder of the packet in her hand, did she look me straight
in the face and begin to ask questions. Because she spoke
Swahili, which was unusual in those days for a Highland
Maasai, I could understand her.

Our talk was oddly feminine and for a time we became as
close as one can only be over a handful of salt in the solitude
of a new-born day, when the Maasai men, carrying their
spears against lions and thieves, had gone out grazing their
herds among far-off lowings, and the European men, in a
hurry to follow fresh buffalo tracks, had forgotten to drink
all their tea.

The only sign left of Paolo that morning was a still steaming
cup, and the squashed stub of his first cigarette. Quick to notice
these traces of a male presence, '*Wapi bwana yako?*' she asked.

'Where is your husband?' But before I could answer about mine, she told me of hers. Her story was typical of all the young beauties of her tribe and her age-group, just after circumcision.

A handsome *moran*, or young warrior, who had already won, by raiding, enough cattle to afford a wife, had shown his interest by offering her a necklace, which she had accepted. Her parents then waited in anticipation for her betrothed to come, according to custom, with his first gift of honey. This, she and the girls circumcised with her – and because of this forever her sisters – mixed with milk and then drank together.

Soon after, vast quantities of honey had been offered by the future groom, and fermented and distilled into a heady liquor that the elders drank amidst celebration. At this stage the young man had been summoned, and was told – may God listen – that his ritual gifts had been accepted and his request granted. No one else might now come to claim his bride.

Her old mother had received a lamb, and her father a calf and cured sheepskins with which to prepare the wedding garment. Two calves and a bull, all white like the cool new moon, had been brought by the groom on the wedding day. As prescribed by custom, they had to be healthy and strong, without marks to scar the soft sun-warmed hides. The unfortunate sacrificial victims of African celebrations – a ram and two hoggets – had been slaughtered, and the wretched ram's fat used as a ceremonial ointment.

On the given day, after the sun had risen like an in-candescent *calabash* on the indigo horizon, her friends sang a high-pitched song of joy, her heart leapt like an impala in the happiness of her special ceremony, and the old women had come. They had doused her with that brew of honey and, helped by her proud mother, they had fixed the ornaments to her leg and ears with elaborate ritual.

I listened, fascinated. The story came in bouts, prompted by questions, and facilitated by half a pound of sugar-cane that she licked casually and with glee, straight from the bag. The sun rose high, and the cicadas' song grew deafening, dry like the sound of twigs beaten together by a thousand hidden hands.

The tall slim woman yawned and stretched. I understood that for today her story was finished. She looked around and her eyes focused on the green cake of soap, drying on a stone, with which Paolo had washed his hands. She pointed at it with a sudden jerk of her chin, emphasizing her desire by pretending to spread it onto her arm and smelling her skin with a beatific smile. I passed it to her and she began to smooth it all over her dry skin like a cream, moaning with pleasure. The flies, uncaring, flew dozily from the restless eyelids, and settled back there immediately.

I asked how many children she had borne. She thought a bit about it, and finally opened three fingers, but, as an afterthought, she slapped her stomach energetically:

'*Mimi ni mimba tena*,' she announced proudly, with a toss of her head. 'I am pregnant again.'

In her voice was a ring, like a fresh bell at dawn.

I was surprised by her thinness and I told her so. She explained that the Maasai were careful not to let pregnant mothers get too fat, as this was regarded as dangerous for the baby. How modern. But pregnant women had the unique privilege of eating meat: an astonishing luxury for this tribe which feed purely on the blood, urine and curdled milk of their cattle. Only stolen meat is normally eaten, never that of their own livestock.

She rose with one fluid movement, and measured me with a cocky, challenging look in her eyes. Suddenly curious she asked:

'*Bwana yako ulilipa ngombe na njau ngapi kwa baba yako*

kuolewa wewe?' 'How many cows and calves did your bwana pay your father for you?'

Slightly humiliated by the inadequacy of our European traditions, I tried to explain that in the land called Ulaia, where I came from, we followed other *desturi*. *Desturi* means custom in Swahili, and is a magic word to unfold the inexplicable. Customs are sacred, unquestionable, instantly accepted without reserve. Often, hiding behind the excuse of my *desturi* had saved me from potentially embarrassing explanations.

It was clear that the woman considered this particular *desturi* undignified, and for a moment it looked so to me also. She made no comment, just lifted her shoulder, almost imperceptibly, to dismiss that incomprehensible European meanness.

With a tinkling of anklets she stood tall, light in her thinness, without leaving any mark on the dust where we had sat together. Then, with a natural grace, she parted the skin garment which, like a peplum, covered her chest, and exposed two pendulous breasts, swollen like ripe oblong gourds. With thumb and index she lifted one, and squeezed it with the expert gesture of the milker. A long opalescent spray spurted out darting inches from my face, hitting the bushes with a sharp noise.

With a proud jerk of her head she invited me to do the same. But before I could admit my defeat, I could detect in her frank, laughing stare a teasing note. A sudden breeze ran unexpected through the treetops, touched our faces and was soon forgotten.

She went away amongst the low sage bushes, without a word, her head held high, as when she had first appeared.

5

MWTUA

Dis aliter visum.*
Virgil, *Aeneid*, II, 428

He was a little man with a perennial grin. His short greying hair, small eyes brightened by a continuous smile, his readiness to obey or volunteer for any work and his intrinsic innocence, were like a peasant-saint's in biblical tales. He had been with me for many years, looking after my house in Nairobi, a reliable fellow respected by all, kind to children and adored by dogs. He was not intelligent, on the contrary perhaps a bit simple, and his sentences often became tangled in a painful stutter, but his good nature and willingness amply made up for his lack of initiative.

I had noticed that recently he had been looking old and become rather forgetful. His stammer had increased, making it more painful for him to answer quickly, and harder for me to understand what he wanted to say. He ironed perfectly but his eyesight seemed to be failing him, and often I found strange garments mixed up with mine and unknown pullovers amongst my shirts.

He looked tired and he shuffled. I began to wonder if he should not retire, and go back to Kitui where he had come from, to look after his grandchildren, and the small *shamba* he had acquired over the years.

He did not want to go; and as if sensing that I was about to

* 'The gods thought otherwise.'

call him to explain that the time had arrived for him to return home and retire in peace, he seemed to double his efforts, to work more and longer hours, as if he wanted to prove to me that, in fact, he still had many years left of active work.

One night, coming back late from a dinner party to my house in Gigiri, instead of the usual guard, a strange little man, trussed up in a too-large nightwatchman's greatcoat, trotted up to the gate and fidgeted endlessly with keys before he finally managed to open it. The oversized helmet on the small grey head had slipped down almost to cover his eyes, but revealed a happy, slightly fanatic grin: it was Mwtua. The *askari* had been taken ill by a sudden attack of malaria, so he had volunteered to help and was spending all night up in the chill, faithfully guarding my house.

Despite all this, I realized that Mwtua had to go, but I wanted to find the right opportunity to tell him.

It was a foggy morning in Nairobi, and when I tried to talk to my ranch on the Laikipia Security network, my radio did not seem to be receiving properly. It had been raining heavily the night before and I wondered if the unusual amount of static meant that a branch had fallen on the aerial. I called Wangari, the maid who was Mwtua's niece, and asked her to go and find a gardener to discover if the aerial was still in the upright position. She was away a few minutes.

'*Ndio*,' she explained. '*Aerial naaunguka, lakini Mwtua nasema yeye nawesa kutanganesa.*'

'Yes. The aerial has fallen, but Mwtua said he can fix it.'

I smiled. It was so typical of him. It was naturally out of the question. The aerial was very high, tied to the top of the tallest tree. The radio people from Wilken had come with a special ladder to do it. It was impossible to reach it otherwise.

'I shall call the maintenance people,' I said to Wangari. 'Please tell Mwtua we will take care of it.'

The telephone was ringing, so I went to answer it. Then I tried to call the radio workshop, but the line was engaged.

I noticed that in the meantime it had started drizzling again. I went to look out of my window. A short wooden ladder was leaning against the Cape chestnut in the middle of the lawn, to which the aerial had been fixed.

A ladder? Why? With a sudden premonition, I reached for my glasses. I looked. Sure enough, amongst the leafy branches, in his green uniform and practically camouflaged, Mwtua was climbing, agile and fast, towards the aerial. I caught my breath: this was impossible. The branches were so thin towards the top, surely they would not support a human body.

The tribesmen of Kisii and Mkamba are forest people; they love working with wood and they know trees. As children they learn to climb for fruit and honey or to steal birds' eggs, while they tend the goats and cattle in the forests. Still, that tree was too high and wet with rain, its branches swaying, unsafe. Mwtua was too old to go climbing. I was about to open the window to call him down, when something about him made me stop.

It was as if a change had come upon him on that tree. His old man's movements had been shed like old skin. A young Mwtua was climbing, alert and nimble, with soft fluid gestures. His thin legs and arms seemed to wrap themselves easily around the branches with a prehensile skill, inherited from bygone arboreal generations. But what was most extraordinary was the transformation of his eyes. They were open and enlarged so that the white part seemed huge, almost phosphorescent, and their still gaze was fixed like an animal's. He reminded me uncannily of a bushbaby I had once kept.

I stopped breathless, looking at him mesmerized.

I did not know that downstairs our *ayah*, Wanjiru, was looking up to Mwtua from the kitchen window with the same apprehension. She told me later that her impressions of Mwtua were identical to mine.

Something had definitely happened to him up that tree.

So deep seemed his transformation, and so remote was he, absorbed in his world of leaves and air, that I was afraid to startle him by opening the window. I decided to attract his attention by rapping on the glass instead, but he did not seem to hear. Then he looked up, like a bird surprised by a strange sound. At that moment the telephone rang in my room again and I went to answer. I was replacing the receiver when I next looked out.

It was raining heavily now, and through the rain I saw the treetop oscillating. Then, in front of my eyes, to my eternal horror, Mwtua's lithe body precipitated, with the slow motion of a nightmare, head first in a shower of leaves, no different from a leaf himself, on to the lawn, to lie there, motionless. A small broken branch fell with him and the radio cable, like a useless liana, swung forlorn in the air. I opened the window to see better.

He lay in a crumpled heap, pathetically small in his green clothes and, with a lump in my throat, I was sure he was dead. No one could have fallen on his head from that height without breaking his neck.

After what seemed a very long stillness, there was a sudden flutter of activity. Like spectators invading the stage after the show has ended, the gardener, the *shamba* woman and Wanjiru ran towards Mwtua as if they had all been waiting to spring into action. At the same time Wangari put her apron over her head, threw up her hands to the sky and, in a new wild voice which sent a chill down my spine, started wailing in an unknown language an eerie and ancient song of mourning.

Wanjiru was on him. I noticed she had kicked her shoes off to run faster.

'Don't touch him!' I screamed from the window, afraid that unskilled handling would make him worse if, by some quirk of fate, he was still alive.

'*Kwisha kufa*?' 'Is he dead?' I called out, praying that this nightmare would finish, hoping to turn back the clock.

'*Badu*!' 'Not yet.' Wanjiru screamed back.

The doctor, then.

I realized that every second could be crucial, and that the right action could make all the difference. With flying fingers, I dialled the home number of the Italian brain-surgeon, a great friend, whom I contact in any emergency. It was a short cut to avoid lengthy explanations to a telephone operator.

'Marieke,' I begged his wife, 'Mwtua has fallen from a tree and I think he is dying. Please tell Renato I am bringing him to Nairobi Hospital now.'

A former nurse herself, she did not waste time with idle questions. I slammed the phone down and ran downstairs.

Surrounded by moaning people, Mwtua was curled up in the foetal position, with his eyes shut. Some mown grass was stuck to his cheek. He looked quite dead.

I felt the great inner silence which anticipates irreversible doom, and in this soundless world I knelt at his side. I forced myself to open one of his eyelids – the skin was cold and clammy – and touched the pupil lightly with a leaf. To my overwhelming relief, the eye contracted, flickered. A shiver ran through his body: he was alive!

Sound crept back in my consciousness, and I became aware of a rasping breathing that came from his chest in bursts. I put my hand on his back and massaged him, calling him softly. Pearly saliva, mixed with grass fragments, frothed from his lips.

We drove him to hospital in the back of my car, wrapped in a blanket, writhing but unconscious, and jerking in his sleep as if he dreamt he was still climbing the tree.

He was put straight into the Intensive Care unit, and the hospital machinery organized by Renato Ruberti began to hum efficiently around him. Blood pressure, temperature, X-rays, physical tests, scans and all kinds of examinations were performed quickly and smoothly. Then Renato looked up at me, while still holding Mwtua's wrist. For a long moment his intelligent eyes behind his spectacles stared into mine before he spoke.

I swallowed.

A broken neck? A fractured skull? A smashed thorax? An irreversible coma? Perennial brain damage? Death in a few minutes?

A sudden grin split his face in two.

'You will not believe it,' he drawled in Italian. 'He has nothing wrong with him at all. Only a slight concussion. The tree was thirty metres tall you said?' He shook his head. 'Not a cracked rib, and not a scratch. He does not even need a plaster.'

The staff howled, accepted his revival as an act of magic, and praised God – who decides who should live and who should die – because in his wisdom he had spared Mwtua, who knew no evil. Masses were celebrated at the mission church back in his village, and special tribal ceremonies of thanksgiving, so that the new and old gods might be appeased.

As a precaution I kept him for a week – during which he mostly slept and was woken regularly only to be hand-fed – under observation in the Intensive Care unit and Special Attention ward at the hospital.

After that a stream of people came to see him. The visitors looked at him in silence and awe, a respect and consideration reserved only for a shaman or *muganga*: they declared there had been a miracle.

In their stories the tree became taller and taller, a holy

force had lifted Mwtua up, a bird had delayed his fall. His adventure gained colours and new details every time it was repeated, as it is normal with legends.

Wanjiru declared that Mwtua had survived because God loved me, and would not allow a tragedy like this to stain my *boma*. Amongst most Kenyan tribes, the people about to pass away were traditionally taken outside their compound, as a house where someone had died was considered impure and should normally be burnt.

Although he had remained inexplicably unhurt, something had happened to Mwtua's head. He wandered around absently, with a beatific expression painted on his face, and nothing seemed to move him. He smiled more than ever, muttered to himself, played with the new puppies a great deal, and sat outside his house in the staff quarters, in a sort of inertia. Tended by his wife, who had come to look after him from the village, he just stared ahead as if contemplating mysterious images within himself.

The doctors suggested that he should do some easy work, and Wanjiru allotted him simple repetitive tasks, like cleaning silver or shoes. He agreed with great enthusiasm, but he held the shoes upside down, polishing the soles, and we soon gave up.

Mwtua went back to his village in the end, where he looked forward to playing with his grandchildren and resting in his *shamba* as becomes an elder.

I was sorry to part with him. But when he came, dressed in a coat which had been Paolo's, to say his long, laborious farewells, shaking my hands and Sveva's again and again as if he did not want to let go, and promising he would come back as soon as possible, we noticed, with amazement, that he had completely lost his stammer.

6

THE BULL SHARK OF VUMA

The old man knew that the shark was dead, but the shark
would not accept it.

Ernest Hemingway, *The Old Man and the Sea*

Out in the Indian Ocean, off the north Kenya coast,
between the fiords of Taka-Ungu and Vipingo, are the
shallows of Vuma.

They are banks of flat, submerged prairies, covered in long
seaweeds growing out of old coral gardens. Restless underwater currents constantly stir the pale green-grey blades of the
plants. They shudder, tossing languid manes, like savannah
grasses bent by the invisible fingers of the Highland wind.
Large shoals of fish of all descriptions come to graze here
from the black depth of the ocean, like the gazelle and
antelope on the Enghelesha plains.

So, too, come the predators.

The waters of Vuma are notorious for the abundance of
sharks, which lurk in the darkness around the shallows, emerging swift and deadly to prey on the foraging herds. Like all
carnivores and scavengers, they are attracted by the jerky,
uneven movements which reveal creatures in distress, and by
the smell of blood, carried through water in thick clouds of
livid red, like a scent on a breeze.

Vuma had acquired a sinister reputation when a number of
dhows had sunk in a series of storms, and the shipwrecked
crews had been devoured by sharks. Such stories were invariably told when someone mentioned the place.

Fast-swimming fish, minor predators, like *cole-cole* and tuna, were known to favour Vuma, and large rock cod lived in coral caves along the edges of the submerged highlands. In a curious way, Vuma was a sea equivalent of Laikipia with its plateau perched on the edge of the Great Rift Valley, and it was naturally irresistible to Paolo, who often went out there from Kilifi with his spear gun, on his rubber dinghy.

He sometimes took a friend or two, but mostly he went with Ben.

Ben was a local fisherman of the Swahili tribe and, like most of them, he followed the Muslim religion, and always wore a tiny embroidered cap. The Swahili, with their Arab blood, distinguished themselves from the Giriama, the most common tribe in Kilifi, of purer Bantu descent.

Ben was small but muscular, with large shoulders on his compact body. Above his short black beard and flat, pointed nose with wide nostrils, his tilted eyes were intelligent and mischievous. He radiated a complete faith in the excellence of his seafaring skills. The arrogance of a race which is noble and proud of its traditions, accompanied a certain roguish indolence which one condoned, as it was mellow, like most coastal sins. It went with the rarefied climate of the coast, the ripe smells of vegetation and humid sands, fruity mangoes, coconut milk and frangipani, *korosho* nut roasted in the evening, fish dried in the sun, spices and damp monsoon. Ben was part of Kilifi, and seeing him meant we had arrived.

With the African's uncanny gift of knowing without being told, and of appearing unexpectedly at the right time from nowhere, within less than an hour of our car arriving at Kilifi, Ben's voice could be heard from the kitchen, greeting my Nairobi staff in his sing-song coastal Swahili. Then the shuffle of his naked feet approached and he appeared, hand stretched out in greeting, calling out our names, asking for a cigarette. We liked him.

Often, his eyes were glazed, his manner slower, dreamier, and the aroma of a reefer drooping from his lips disclosed that again Ben was smoking *bhang*. This habit which, he maintained, made his sight sharper and helped him to see fish better under water, was accepted as part of him, and won him the nickname of 'Bhangy-Ben'.

He was an excellent, natural fisherman, with a genuine passion for the ocean. More than anything he enjoyed going out looking for marlin, and he was unbeatable at spotting the shoals of sardines signalled on the shimmering horizon by fluttering flights of feeding seagulls; they were infallibly followed by hungry *bonito* tuna, and these often by sailfish or marlin.

He knew the secrets of the tides, and the habits of fish, rather like the trackers of the Highlands knew the game they were stalking.

In fact, I always associated Ben with Luka, our inimitable Tharaka hunter and Paolo's companion of countless adventures, who knew how to think like the buffalo. He could find them in thick bush just by listening for the tick bird, just, one might have thought, by sniffing the air with his sensitive nostrils.

Both had the same self-assurance which came from the total mastery of their skills and complete understanding of their background, the Indian Ocean and the Highland savannah. Each in his own way believed his presence to be – and possibly it was – indispensable to any of Paolo's expeditions.

Ben had presided over most of Paolo's fishing adventures: the time of the giant rock cod, and the time of the black marlin which Paolo caught without fishing chair or belt, standing for hours in a rubber dinghy oscillating on the ocean's swell, and which won him his first fishing trophy.

The house where we stayed in Kilifi belonged to an Italian friend who lived in a hacienda in Argentina. He had only been there once in ten years, while it was being built. With Latin generosity he gave us the unlimited use of it, and we regarded it as our home at the coast.

The garden was an unruly profusion of bougainvillea and solanum, with some palms and the most magnificent baobab, a giant of perfectly harmonious proportions, with which I felt great affinity. I gave it a soul, like all trees, and a soul that I liked. I spent many hours each day sitting with my back to it, thinking my thoughts, writing my diary, waiting for Paolo and Emanuele to come back from fishing. It was a time of peace, in which I managed to catch some intuition and hold some passing verses before they flew off with the wind.

Like Ulysses in other seas, and all the sailors ever, Paolo and Ema so often had an adventure to tell. The giant cod harpooned with Lorenzo Ricciardi; the dolphins who had joined in an ocean dance; the sailfish which had gone with the bait; the *upupa* that had flown from nowhere and landed on Paolo's hair.

And then there was the time of the bull shark at Vuma.

Paolo had gone fishing for *cole-cole* at Vuma one morning of January, with his brother and a friend. It was still the time of his passion for spear fishing. Without bottles, with only his mask and snorkel, he dived confidently and deep. I feared always that his lungs would burst; but he would come up after what to me seemed ages, not panting at all, with a fish on his spear and a blue look of triumph on his tanned face.

Ben could not go out that day. He had come in early to announce that another of his children had been born in the night to his sweet Swahili wife, another boy; amongst Muslims this was a serious matter and cause for much ceremony and celebration. As he could not go, he advised that everyone should stay at home, or join me in my planned shopping expedition to Mombasa harbour.

Ben did not like it when he could not go out fishing with Paolo, and always made sure everyone knew of his disapproval — as if his presence were essential for every adventure to be faultless, and unknown evils would befall the boat and its occupants in his absence.

He often spoke of the capricious *djinns* who fly with the sea winds, to bring mischief and to create chaos amongst the incautious, the unfaithful and the unaware. He boasted often of episodes when, in his opinion, only his presence had exorcised dangers. Once the boat had not capsized when he and Paolo caught three marlins in quick succession; only they had succeeded in getting enough bait that day, and in finding the yellow-fin tuna in August, when the fishermen who are worth their salt never venture too far to tempt fate beyond the coral reef — because the monsoon blows with such rage that all fish seem to disappear, and only the giant squids of the depths remain, and the lobsters which have no soul.

Unworried by these predictions of gloom, Paolo and his friends went out happily, leaving Ben still standing in the doorway, shaking his head and mumbling. I went to Mombasa to buy *kangas* and baskets at the bazaars.

When I returned I could feel something had happened even before I got out of my car; no one came to greet me. There was nobody around. From the empty kitchen door a cat looked at me impassively. It was a strange cat, which I had not seen before. The friend who owned the Kilifi Plantations, and was a true mine of all coastal legends, had told me the Giriama never chase away a stray cat begging at their door, as they believe it is the returning soul of a departed person. With this thought in mind I went to look over the cliff.

Down on the beach, I could see a small crowd gathered on the shore. Surrounded by the children, our friends, the staff and quite a few passers-by, Paolo was crouching close to the biggest fish I had ever seen. Its white upturned belly offered to the sun was interrupted by the ugly line of a mouth like a trap, set with curved teeth. A triangular fin protruded from its grey back. Defenceless and inert, it still appeared dangerous.

It was dead and it was a shark.

And so came the story.

From the depth of Vuma, after a full morning of fishing, Paolo had swum back to the surface, his prey, a *cole-cole*, still alive and moving, tied at his belt. Before emerging, the instinctive alarm which saves the life of the hunter warned Paolo to look down; and below him, from the ink-black darkness, a fish was approaching fast, looming bigger and bigger, as if magnified rapidly by an invisible lens.

When it was a few yards from Paolo it stopped and shivered, collecting itself before springing to the attack with a jerk. The snout slid back like a mask, exposing horrid long fangs in two circular rows; the small round eyes focused on Paolo, cold and expressionless.

It was a bull shark, of the kind which attacks more often than any other. The one known to eat sailors.

Too late to climb out of the water, too late to let his wounded fish go. In the blue, alone with the shark, Paolo had lost no time to think. He grabbed his loaded spear gun, placed it between his legs, and pointed it straight at the shark's head. At the moment it was about to strike, he let the shot go.

The head of the spear penetrated the shark's forehead at a right angle. The shark stopped, writhing, and with over-whelming relief Paolo watched him sink. He sank like stone, growing smaller and smaller, almost now out of sight in the depths, pulling with him metres and metres of rope and the floating balloon attached to it.

Elated, adrenalin pumping high, safe, Paolo climbed into

the boat, from which his friends had been watching in breathless alarm. Together, with great difficulty, they hauled in the huge rigid beast. He was almost as long as the boat, heavy, his snout still contracted, his glassy eyes expressionless. They forced his mouth open exposing the fangs, and fingered them, exclaiming at their size. Roping the shark to the boat so they could tow him back to show us, they prepared to start the engine.

As for buffaloes and for lions, there is always another life for a shark. Before the engine sputtered and ignited, a long shiver shook the fish. The wrinkled snout relaxed, and he struggled to loosen his bonds. Then he started to swim off with immense strength, pulling the dinghy, and Paolo, and his friends with him. A scene out of *Jaws*.

Here Paolo paused, looking around for effect.

On the Kilifi beach at high noon, with the reef shimmering and sparkling on the horizon, the tiny waves of low tide gently lapping the shore, and the palm leaves rustling in the breeze, we could have heard a coconut fall on the sand. Paolo's audience waited without breathing.

He continued. In the fragile rubber dinghy, pulled wildly over the sea, pandemonium ensued, as we could all imagine. Finally, with some difficulty, they managed to recover themselves; the engine sprang to life, gained momentum and pulled the boat in the opposite direction.

Weakened, gradually the fish gave up. Dragged backwards, the water entered its gills and it drowned. It took them hours to drive back on a sunny, tumultuous sea, with their heavy cargo not quite dead and their boat made of rubber.

Nobody could tell a story better than Paolo. In his words the adventure took on the colours and sounds of an epic sea saga; Homer and the sirens of myth paled beside this real-life drama. The crowd and I hung from his lips, spell-bound.

Finally the shark was heaved laboriously on to the back of

a pick-up and driven in glory to the Mnarani Club. The fish scale there, good for marlin and sailfish, proved to be too small, so with a cortege of supporters Paolo and his friends went on to the farm scale at the Kilifi Plantations.

The shark weighed 532 pounds. Someone took several photographs, one of which appeared in the *East African Standard,* with the caption: 'Mr Paulo Gullman, a fisherman from upcountry, with a 532lbs man-eater Bull shark.'

'Quite remarkable,' commented one of the orthodox fishing club members, mumbling into his pipe. 'What a shame he did not use a rod. It could have been an all-Africa record.'

This adventure became the talk of Kilifi for weeks.

The only person who did not seem impressed was Ben. '*Kama mimi alikua huko nikushika samaki, hio papa awessi kukaribia,*' he grumbled, tossing his cap. 'If I had been there, that shark would have never dared to attack.'

Nobody cared to deny it, and perhaps he was right.

7

LANGAT

When we build, let us think that we build forever.
John Ruskin, *The Seven Lamps of Architecture*

A woman approached on the road at noon, old, bent, dressed in rags. She walked up to me with slow shuffling steps, bare knotted feet covered in dust. It was dry and hot at Kuti. Again we had missed the rains.

I looked at her: haggard face, colourless handkerchief tied around her grey head. Long earlobes, all her teeth virtually missing. Yet perhaps she was not that old. She greeted me. I answered and waited.

'I am hungry,' she said in halting Swahili. 'I come from far.'

'Who are you?' I reached into my pocket.

A vague reminiscence stirred, of eyes which were once brighter, a lost twinkle, a pride, the dignity of being married to a good man.

'I was Langat's wife.'

The memories came back, like running children.

When we decided to build the house, Paolo called up the *fundis*, and I went to meet them.

'Here is Arap Langat,' he said; and I found myself looking into clear, grey and unblinking wise eyes.

Langat was short and almost plump. His cropped hair was very white, his dark face round, with a small nose, wide cheekbones and even white teeth untarnished by age and chewing tobacco. His earlobes had been stretched – in Nandi custom – and hung down to his shoulders.

What struck me most, apart from his unwavering eyes, which looked straight, piercingly into mine, as if to measure me up, was his air of self-assured dignity, and the composure which emanated from him. I learned later that this came from the knowledge of his competence and the versatility in his job, which he liked and in which he took great pride.

Nguare and Lwokwolognei were his assistants. Nguare was a middle-aged Kikuyu, whose speciality was woodwork. His name – inappropriately, as he was a quiet, serious man with slow feet, usually awkwardly wrapped in ill-fitting clothes – was the Swahili word for francolin, an alert, scuttling little creature, always dashing into the shrubs at the side of the road. Extremely slow and precise in his work, Nguare had the peculiar habit of repeating always the last word of a phrase. He had a pale brown-yellow face in great contrast with the deep ink-black of Arap Langat and of Lwok-wolognei.

Often one finds in an African features that are startlingly similar – but for the shade of his skin – to a European equivalent. Nguare was the practically identical brown version of a long-lost friend in Veneto, Alvise: and the African's smiling face never failed to remind me of that other, sur-rounded in the dreaminess of my memory by the drifting fogs of the Laguna.

The trio was completed by Lwokwolognei, junior, and still an apprentice at that time. With the vertiginous thinness found only in Turkana, he had a lean lustrous face, in which the only eye shone with a doubly vivid light, as if to compensate for the other, lost we never knew how. The eyelid perennially closed over the empty socket, gave him, when seen in profile, the melancholic look of a secretary bird. Lwokwolognei did a bit of everything, from masonry to carpentry, but his real passion was wood carving, at which he excelled, displaying in it a rare imagination and a naive artistry.

He had a bright young wife called Mary, industrious in embroidering goatskins with intricate patterns of beads and shells. But one day she died in childbirth and Lwokwolognei was seldom seen to smile again.

We had moved from Italy to Kenya a few years before and only recently acquired this vast piece of land in the Highlands, on the edge of the Great Rift Valley. It was still early days here in Laikipia, when everything had yet to be learnt, yet to be built, and we were trying to give physical substance to the shape of our dreams.

Constructing our house was one of the first steps, and as Paolo, in this new venture, had so much else to attend to, the task of deciding what we needed and of supervising its construction was left largely to me.

I looked around and found the objects that nature had created and left, like a generous, careless artist, exposed for us to discover and to enjoy. I loved to use these local materials, rocks from the river and boulders from the hills, logs cut from the forest's red cedar, or old twisted olive trunks, bleached by generations of suns and sculpted into fantastic forms by the insuperable art of strong winds.

Langat knew what he could achieve and was able to put into practice my architectural whims. He let his dormant, instinctive, tribal fantasy prevail, yet blend with the stereo-typed European building notions that had been hammered into him in the days of his apprenticeship. In this combination of inspired intuition and acquired skill lay the roots of his excellence.

He was infallible in finding exactly what I wanted. After the first few times, when we had driven out together, looking for a special shape in the stones or grain in the trees, he was quick to pick up and interpret this new European extravagance: the preference for rough rocks to neat smooth cement; for old twisted *mutamayo*, forgotten by termites or too hard for them to devour, to planks of sawn factory timber; for grass thatch and palm roofing, reminders of breezes and savannah, instead of the shining corrugated iron sheets which today scar the African plains.

We began to build the main house with its sitting room and verandah. When some difficult spot was reached, Langat and I had a thinking session, considering the problem to-gether, and together finding aesthetically appropriate solu-tions. A stone added to, or taken from a partition, a lower rather than a higher wall, a steeper slope to the roof; a door encased in a wooden frame to blend with the walls; a crafty shelf; the proportions of the raised fireplace, in the Venetian tradition, but with cedar pillars; the curve of a sunken bath. Arap Langat and I shared the pleasure of building something which felt good. We went into the Enghelesha forest to search for a long dead tree to make into a post, for olive wood for our dining table, or for a huge flat stone to fashion into a seat.

When the house was finally built, the *makuti* roof thatched, the furniture put in place, the brass polished, our antique Ethiopian carpets arranged on the red tiled floors and flower-ing plants placed in copper pots, I felt a great sense of achieve-ment. Yet I soon realized there was something not quite right, something disturbing and indefinable, some creeping noise which filtered down from the palm thatch and to which I dared not give a name. But Langat did.

'*Memsaab*,' he gravely told me one day, pointing a short chubby finger to the roof, '*iko nyoka kwa rufu.*' 'There are worms in the roof.'

I looked at him pleadingly. He went on.

'*Wewe hapana sikia sawti? Hawa nakula pole-pole.*' 'Don't you hear their noise? They are eating slowly, slowly.'

In the silence – or was it the rustle of the hibiscus in the breeze – I thought I heard the chomping of a million minute mouths eating away at the roof overhead. I touched the wooden frame made of *poriti* posts cut out of mangrove trees from Lamu. I shook it, and an infinitesimally fine powder fell, formed, alarmingly, of thousands of round pellets of digested thatch. It was a horrible thought and I had to tell Paolo.

When he chose, Paolo could be totally detached. Admitting the presence of worms in our roof would mean taking cumbersome, messy, and, most of all, immediate action to remove them.

'No, I do not think so,' he said, with a studied indifference that could not fool me. He too had been listening. He shook a beam unconvincingly and the powder fell, but with no real evidence of actual worms.

'Dust. I think it is some sort of dust from the brittle leaves.' We both knew there was more to it than this, and Langat knowingly shook his head. But for a time we left it at that.

Yet in the pauses of conversation, when the silence of the embers followed the jolly crackling of the fire, we thought we heard the haunting noise of countless creatures chewing away at our house.

Before long we had to face it.

'What's this?' asked Jasper Evans phlegmatically one afternoon when he had dropped in for a drink, peering amused into his beer mug. We looked. A fat pale worm swam in it, frantically.

When another worm plopped in my mother's soup that same night, Paolo surrendered to the evidence that our roof was infested by them, and decided to spray it.

Assisted by Langat and his team of *fundis*, perched on the yellow tractor especially driven from Enghelesha, Paolo, like an ancient squire in a modern tournament, mounted on an improbable *destriero*, manoeuvred the hose-pipe, aiming the potent jet of insecticide towards the roof.

Inside, all the furniture had been removed and the house was once again bare.

The exercise took a few days, but the stench lingered for weeks. At night we ate where we slept, in our bedroom, and during the day under the large yellow fever tree on the lawn. The roof never recovered its original well-combed appearance, and the children laughed, comparing it to an unkempt, windblown hairstyle.

The years went by, and destiny struck twice. On both occasions Langat was in the group of men who came to fetch the grave stones from the bush. Strange to stand straight, alone, watching the crowd of ranch people – twenty? thirty? – trying to lift them from the place where they had lain since the beginning of the earth. Two boulders – two among millions – chosen to leave the parched bush to mark forever the heads of my men in a garden of green and flowers. Langat oversaw these operations, a small erect figure with a greying round head, and swishing pendulous lobes swinging at its sides.

Since those times, he developed the habit of taking my hand in his for long moments whenever we met, holding it there without shaking it. His slate grey, shining eyes did not smile, but he managed to infuse into them a depth of liking for me which gave me a warm pleasure, as if they were dark friendly ponds, mirroring my smile.

There was a fine dignity and poise about Langat, a quiet certainty of his worth. He looked old, wise, and it was with great surprise that we learnt one day he had taken a new wife. She was a fat girl, with small strange slanting eyes, almost oriental, young enough to be twice his daughter. She spent most of the time standing around the office block at Centre, chatting away with the other wives, knitting complicated patterns in bright yarns, looking well pregnant.

Langat went about pleased with himself. His old wife, as is the custom, went back to look after his *shamba* in Nandi.

In recent years, I decided to add to the original hut overlooking the Mukutan stream, now worn by weather and termites, to make it into a permanent retreat for me, a place where I could go and rest alone, and find again my inner voice.

Langat put all his heart into this task: a free house with no doors or windows, open to winds and suns and moons. Perched on a cliff, like a nest, it followed the contour of the landscape, watching over the hills and the green bush, soon to be black with buffalo. It looked down on the stream, beloved by hammerkops and woolly-necked storks, and listened to the frogs and giant toads and the million crickets. Together, Langat and I built in it a sunken bath patterned with shells, a four-poster bed of dead trees rising from the rocks, and a roof to host wandering swallows.

Then one day, when the construction was about to be finished, Langat was taken sick, of malaria they thought, and he was sent to the hospital in Ol Kalau. Before he left he wanted a photograph, of himself, Lwokwolognei and me, within the enclosure of the stone bed-to-be.

A few days later I flew up to Laikipia from Nairobi in the middle of the week with an Italian friend, who had come on a brief visit. I took him to the Mukutan, to have a look at the progress of our work. Nobody spoke when we got out of the car. They lifted their heads, and lowered them again, without a word.

Lwokwolognei was plastering a stone seat, with slow careless strokes. He looked up, his one eye full of pain, like a wounded antelope. I saw with a sense of shock that something sad, terribly sad, had happened. I put my hand firmly on his shoulder, so that he had to turn his long thin neck and look up at me with his one good eye, the empty socket gaping pitifully, as if he were lost, or angry at some evil and incomprehensible god's wrongdoing.

'*Kitu gani? Kitu gani naharibu roho yako?*' 'What is it? What has happened to spoil your heart?' I inquired quietly.

They had all stopped working and waited, with that bated silence that we grow to understand, living in Africa. Only then did I realize something was missing: Langat was not back. And even before Lwokwolognei spoke I knew his answer.

Langat's malaria had been a minor stroke which had been followed by a terminal one. I would never see him again.

'Langat is dead. His hour has struck,' Lwokwolognei said simply, and he went back to work.

I felt in my own heart that familiar squeeze, anger, sense of loss. Another tie with my past gone forever. Another friend passed on. Those wise twinkling eyes, those stretched lobes, his face when Ema had died. Yet what he had built will be there for as long as there are hills.

'*Ni shauri ya Mungu.*' 'It is the will of God,' – the African explanation of the unexplainable and of the unavoidable – I murmured, small and vulnerable in the presence of infinity and I felt, again, the wisdom and comfort of believing it.

'*Ni shauri ya Mungu,*' Lwokwolognei repeated.

They all nodded, in sad patience. Thus, in Africa, one accepts the strokes of fate. I shook all their hands in silence and drove off. My Italian friend had understood nothing.

8

THE STORY OF NUNGU NUNGU

For Gilfrid

They left a great many odd little foot-marks all over the bed, especially little Benjamin.

Beatrix Potter, *The Tale of Benjamin Bunny*

In the early days at Laikipia, I decided to carve a vegetable garden and an orchard out of a shrubby area behind the house. It was close enough to the kitchen to ensure some sort of protection from the various pests which would attempt to eat the produce.

Elephant loved bananas and oranges, gazelles lettuces, spinach and broccoli, moles fennel, potatoes, carrots and all the tubers. An astonishing variety of little vermin devoured just about anything, and birds wiped out everything else, including, thank God, insects.

An ingenious and noisy – if primitive and rather messy – contraption of tins rattling on poles, vibrating strings, floating net and long strips of plastic that flapped in the breeze, was devised to discourage the birds. It was set up, tested, and discarded in turns. It was supervised by a formidable *spaventapasseri*. Dressed in one of Paolo's old jackets and topped with one of my mother's forgotten straw hats, it conducted, like a veritable wizard, this ill-assorted orchestra from the height of an old broomstick.

Nasturtiums and tagetes were planted around the vegetable beds to discourage the flying insects with their effluvia; ashes from the fireplace were scattered round tomatoes and courgettes, and hay round strawberries, to deter crawling

46

1. The house and garden at Kuti

2. Kuki and Sveva

3. Emanuele and a pet young agama

4. Tigger

5. Ol Ari Nyiro: cheetah at Nagiri dam

6. The Pokot women come to Kuti

7 & 8. A hoopoe flew on to Paolo's head

9. Ben, Paolo and the Bullshark of Vuma

10. Sveva and Meave at Ol Ari Nyiro Springs

11. Elephant seen from the treetop below Paolo's dam

12. Elephants drinking at a dam

13. Ekiru Mirimuk guarding the hills

14. Kuki and baby rhino

15. Lake Turkana

bugs; while a wire net, practically dik–dik proof, was set on posts round the whole compound.

At night the Tharaka *askari* stood guard with a primitive catapult, of ancient design and time-proven accuracy – identical, I suspected, to the one David had used to kill Goliath. Like his biblical predecessor confronting the mythical giant, Sabino, creeping in the shadows, knocked round stones smartly on the backs of any elephant approaching the guava. Outraged trumpeting piercing the night meant he had hit the target, and became a picturesque feature of our evening meals, and cause of bewildering entertainment for our European guests.

The elephant did not seem to mind.

One night an extraordinary commotion made us run to look. A young elephant, one of a group of fifty which had lately been foraging on my bananas, had fallen into the septic tank. His companions were pushing him out. As always on these occasions, nobody could find a camera, but next day we ordered an electric fence.

A wire mesh cage was eventually erected to keep away even the most daring mouse birds, and my vegetable garden became an unconquerable fortress. Yet . . .

'*Muivi alikuja kukula mboga.*' 'A thief has come to eat the cabbages,' the gardener Seronera announced mournfully one morning, holding out to me a half-eaten cabbage leaf. Cabbages took ages to grow.

'He dug a tunnel below the enclosure,' he offered by way of explanation. We had not thought of this. He shook his head in knowing admiration.

'What! That thing is quite clever.' He produced a long quill, striped cream and brown, grinning.

'*Ni nungu nungu: yeye napenda mboga saidi.*' 'It is a porcupine: he is wild about cabbages.'

I went to look, and sure enough, in the crumbly fat earth,

lovingly manured and watered, little prints like a toddler's hand marked the soil. A large hole had been dug below the netting, and the tracks went inexorably to and from the cabbage patch. The thief had helped himself liberally. Another quill, like a signature, was stuck in the softened earth. It was a porcupine sure enough.

The net was repaired, but a few mornings later, Nungu Nungu came again. Another few cabbages were munched away. The little child's marks told the tale. This time we dug the netting deeper into the soil. It did not seem to help. Some weeks, and quite a few cabbages later, I decided to catch the thief with a trap. We already had one.

Nguare and Lwokwolognei had built it, to catch a leopard that had been killing sheep and which we let go in Samburu Park. The leopard had not liked being trapped, and had snarled furiously from behind the canvas with which we had covered the cage to protect him from the light and the unsettling sight of humans. How deep had been his bronchial roar. How much its sound had been for me the voice of Africa, and of all the unknown, untamed world around me.

This cage was sturdy, made out of thick timber, with heavy duty wire sides and a trapdoor, craftily connected to a bait. The door would slide down with a bang capturing the thief when he took the lure. Formidable, I thought, for a porcupine. In the leopard's case, the bait had been the almost rotten carcass of a sheep. This time, it was a cabbage.

We set the trap meticulously, careful not to leave any human scent to reveal the plot to Nungu Nungu's suspicious mind. The most inviting fresh cabbage was placed in the middle. Nungu Nungu did not resist. Next morning, he was there.

Nungu Nungu was huge, with brown liquid eyes. He was covered in long quills which stood out, erect, while, at our approach, the hollow ones of his tail made a curious dry noise of frantically shaken castanets. He was pacing his prison, trailing his spiky train with the hauteur of an outraged great Red Indian chief. The closer we came, the louder, more threatening, the noise seemed to grow. But, all in all, he appeared remarkably quiet for what must have been a disconcerting experience.

And he had eaten the cabbage.

We put the cage on my pick-up, not without difficulty, and drove off. I stopped in a bushy area several miles away. With the help of all the gardeners, our tracker Luka, and a grinning Emanuele we lowered the cage with great caution in the shade of some shrubs. Then I opened the door, and walked some distance away.

After a time, feeling safe, a little face peered out, and we watched Nungu Nungu zig-zag rapidly off through the undergrowth.

A few nights after this episode, the cabbages were eaten once more. We set the trap, and again, we found a porcupine inside next morning.

How could we tell porcupines apart? Seronera suggested it might be Nungu Nungu's mate; perhaps there was a family of them?

But Colin, my ranch manager, said it would be the same one, who had come back. Leopard, like some domestic cats, were known to have walked hundreds of kilometres back to their territory. It did not seem possible, yet who could know what instinct might not guide this creature back home?

This time I sent the pick-up to release him further away still, well over the Ol Morani boundary, on a vast grassy *mbogani* dotted with low *carissa* bushes, a long long way even for a determined Nungu Nungu.

'*Kwisha rudi.*' 'He has come back,' announced Seronera some while after.

Was he really the same one? It was hard to believe.

Driven by curiosity, determined to solve the riddle, I found a tin of paint, and, through the wire mesh, sprayed the crackling quills a vivid green.

This time I drove the cage up to the Pokot boundary, with the usual assortment of giggling spectators in the back.

At sunset, when the shadows are long, and the flocks of guinea fowl settle on the highest branches of the acacia to sleep, and the swifts dart low piercing the sky with their screeches, and the tree-frogs wake up with a sound of fresh bells, we set a green Nungu Nungu free over the boundary line.

'*Kwisha rudi tena*,' murmured in awe Seronera a week later. He held a long quill, partly covered in bright green paint. I laughed and laughed. We all did. Such persistent, pig-headed greed commanded respect.

After all, I never liked cabbages. We tried artichokes, instead.

9

THE TALE OF
TWO BUSHBABIES

And the elves also,
Whose little eyes glow
Like sparks of fire, befriend thee.

Robert Herrick,
The Night Piece, To Julia

Nights in Africa are never silent. If you listen carefully an entire orchestra of diverse sounds and secret voices reaches you from the grass and the hills, the dunes, the ponds and the trees. And if you look for the unseen creatures which animate the night you can often, for a moment, glimpse their eyes, piercing the blackness. If they seem to dance high upon the treetops like mischievous elves, faster than your sight can catch them, and if their voices sound like the whine of a child lost in the forest, probably they are bushbabies. Related to lemurs and monkeys, nocturnal, arboreal, they feed on insects and fruit.

The first I met was Koba. From the dark of the store you could only see his eyes: shiny and round, and in some odd way disturbing. Opening the door I brought the sun with me, and in its white blinding light the pupils of his huge eyes contracted, and the irises stood out dull in the tiny face.

He was clasping the shoulder of the man who wanted to sell him; a string of plaited palm leaves circled his narrow waist and underlined the difference between the upper part of his body – slim, with frail arms – and the lower half, with powerful, muscled legs, ready to jump. He looked like a small kangaroo with a squirrel's tail.

I had never seen a bushbaby so close before. The nights at the coast are full of their raucous screams, as they jump from branch to branch on the baobabs. But during the day they are invisible, and only after sunset is it possible, with much patience, to discover their lithe bodies amongst the leaves.

It was easy to catch them.

The local people in those days hung from the baobab branches dishes of a strong sweet beer, made out of coconut and honey, and the bushbabies could not resist its heady aroma. Dead drunk in the green dawn, still in a stupefied sleep, they would lie scattered at the foot of the majestic trees, like the moths they had not managed to eat. The villagers would harvest them easily, and they would try to sell them, tied to a length of palm twine, to passing tourists at the ferry-boat jetties along the creeks.

Koba had been captured by chance. He was still a baby, and had been grasping his dozy mother's back when she had been caught. But she had managed to escape somehow, and the man, who was the swimming pool attendant at the hotel in Diani, had brought the baby to the pool store, where during the day he was kept amongst bath towels, deck chairs and rubber flippers. It was there that Emanuele had discovered him and, in dismay, had begged me to buy him and let him go.

Now the young bushbaby stood trembling, uncertain and fragile like a bird who cannot yet fly. He looked strange, somehow alien.

Overcoming an instinctive, inexplicable repugnance, I reached out to take him. His small black hands were damp and gluey, with the wrinkled knuckles and spatulate nails of an old child; they were cold in the great sun. He jumped to my shoulder and grabbed my neck, and against my hair I sensed the pulse of his small frightened life, seeking protection. I suddenly felt for him, and for a few shillings he became ours.

We called him Koba, a contraction of the Swahili name Komba, and Emanuele and my young stepdaughters were deliriously happy of his gift. My condition was that in time we should let him go.

We tried. We had learnt that initially his mother had come to look for him many times, piercing the starry night with shrieks of pain, leaping from the palm trees on to the flowering shrubs round his prison. Emanuele put him out on a branch at dusk, and waited several evenings for her to return: but she never did, nor did Koba dare to go off on his own either.

Finally we decided to keep him with us.

When the holiday came to an end, we had to leave the coast and return to Nairobi, but there were bushbabies there, and we hoped that one day we could let Koba go free.

He was a delightful pet. He slept curled in a ball in some hidden recess, on a bookshelf or above a window, and woke up to eat the fruit or the insects which the children constantly caught for him. He often came to us hoping for a special morsel, a sip of the sweet warm tea that he loved, his head slightly tilted as if waiting, his round velvety eyes immense, attentive and oddly unblinking. He took our gifts with dainty fingers, and ate them slowly, holding them with both hands like biscuits.

There was something curiously disquieting about him, and I could never fix my eyes on his without unease, as if he were the memory of a lost identity, lingering in the subconscious, like the faded image of an unknown prehistoric ancestor.

Apart from the repellent habit of urinating on his hands and leaving a trail of humid scent which smelt strongly of liquorice and overripe papaya, Koba was quiet and gentle. But our dogs were unsettled by his presence, pricked their ears at him, and growled in warning – or was it perhaps jealousy at our attentions – whenever they saw him grasping a curtain and repairing to a high shelf inside the house. We realized that we could not leave him at large on his own and, much as I hated it, we had to build a vast cage for him, enclosing enough leafy branches so that he could jump about safely whenever we went out.

One day I came back to find the cage door open. The leaves seemed disturbed and Koba was no longer there. The children called him that evening, and the evening after, and many more. Emanuele put out ripe mangoes, passion fruit, fat glow-worms and grasshoppers on the forks of branches to tempt him. But Koba never came back. To console Emanuele I told him that Koba was probably happy and had found a companion. Yet I knew that he could not possibly cope on his own.

It was an afternoon a week or so later, and it had been raining. Leaves covered the grass below the forest trees in my garden at Gigiri. Termites on their nuptial flights filled the air with their rich, merry buzz, and I inhaled deeply the humid air which smelt of rich earth, humus, and growing new shoots, while I walked around my garden with a friend who had come for tea.

It looked like a discarded *peluche*, a toy of a lost childhood forgotten out in the rain, a kitten drowned in a Venetian canal, its wet hair sticking pitifully to a miserable, minute body. It lay next to the tree which it had not managed to climb. My friend gasped in horror.

Koba's tail seemed made out of damp feathers, but what haunted me for nights were his eyes: open and glassy, totally white, with no more pupils, they were like winter mirrors that had been dulled, and reflected no more.

We buried him quickly behind the staff quarters, so that Emanuele would not know.

The children continued to call him in the evenings, from time to time, and on a few occasions they thought they saw him leaping in the treetops like a fairy. I never dared to tell them what had really happened. We all missed him. The memory remained of the faint smell of liquorice and overripe fruit which was his, and a sadness like a sense of guilt.

And for a time I could not hug my large dogs, although I knew that they were not to blame, really.

Years later, one afternoon in Laikipia, a plane landed at Kuti and a couple of friends strolled over to the house. Something seemed to move under the girl's jacket. Round eyes, unblinking, peered at me from its folds and brought back the memories.

'It is a young bushbaby,' said Davina. 'Could you please keep him: the others have rejected him; they wounded him in a fight.'

Davina's mother had a family of semi-tame bushbabies living in and around her house in Karen.

'He is too young you know. They are territorial and they are going to kill him.' She gazed up at my tall roof of *makuti*.

'He will just love it here; please take him.'

I looked at all my dogs. The image of Koba's white eyes chilled me for a moment. The bushbaby grasped my hand with tiny sticky fingers.

'Why not? Provided you accept that I shall never put him in a cage.' I shivered at the thought. 'Bushbabies should be free to escape. He may find a friend.'

I knew we had bushbabies in Laikipia, particularly in the Enghelesha forest, although I had never seen one yet.

I called him Charlie. He spent the days sleeping in the tiny wooden bird house the *fundi* built for him, and which I hung from the tallest post on my verandah. In the evenings, when the bats filled the air with their screeches, he woke up and went to feed from a bowl of fruit and cake crumbs and honey. Then he crept out to the windows, trying to catch the odd night-insect attracted by the spotlights reflected in the glass.

He loved my ceiling. The *poriti* rafters made from mangrove poles, and the palms fronds of the *makuti* roof may have still smelt of the coast from which his ancestors came, and provided him with the most exceptional palaestra for his jumps, mad exercises and somersaults. Every night he performed there for us, pirouetting wildly above our heads in daring leaps like a circus acrobat.

During dinner he used to approach the dining room table in expectation of some special gift of a choice tid-bit. He loved chocolate soufflé, at which Simon, my Turkana cook, excelled. And when he could smell hot vanilla, he waited for me to stand calling him softly, holding out to him a piece which he ate politely, looking at me intently, with his thoughtful round eyes.

One should really never ever keep wild pets in a tame home. It is impossible to give them the constant care and attention they need. They develop habits that they should not have, and become dependent and over-trusting. Usually it all ends in tears.

I went to Europe for ten days, and when I came back Charlie was no longer there. In the evenings, during my absence, there had been none of the lights to which he was used, none of the animation, the activity, or the human life, unfolding below in front of his curious eyes.

Bushbabies are gregarious and perhaps, as he had felt lonely, he had wandered off. An eagle owl, that eats kittens, squirrels and rats, had been seen often, flapping its heavy wings in the moonlit garden, its hooded eyes scanning the flowered bushes for a sudden stir. The first night I came back I spotted its large sinister shadow perched on the yellow fever tree in the middle of my lawn, and its raucous scream of hunger before the hunt sent a cold shiver down my spine.

I felt sure that he had taken Charlie. I was sad, and so was Emanuele, then a teenager with long legs and wise eyes, and also Sveva, a chubby toddler who had adored watching Charlie's antics, and giggled at his passion for vanilla and chocolate desserts.

It was perhaps a year or so later that Rocky Francombe, the manager's wife, whose house at Centre was about eight kilometres away from mine, told me with great excitement:

'We saw a bushbaby last night. He came over to the house while we were having our pudding, and climbed onto the verandah beams as if waiting for us to notice him. He ate some of the passion fruit mousse from my hands. Today Andrew found him asleep in a bougainvillea bush, next to our bird bath. He had taken over an abandoned starling's nest. I think he is Charlie.'

She smiled at me.

'He was not alone. There was another bushbaby asleep with him.'

10

THE PENDULUM

Home is the sailor, home from the sea.

Robert Louis Stevenson, *Underwoods*,
I, XX, 'Requiem'

He was a pleasant man with old-fashioned manners, tall and still good-looking in his middle age. His greying hair, impeccably parted on one side, set off his tanned skin, regular features and dark, lively eyes.

Like Dickie Mason, the father of Emanuele's friend Charlie, he had been in the Royal Navy, and of the dashing young officer he still kept the upright bearing and chivalrous ways. He loved sailing and when we went to Kilifi he often spoke of long-gone adventures of the sea.

He excelled at telling stories and had, in fact, a fascinating and seemingly unending repertoire of legends and tales of the coast. Most had to do with the magic beliefs, fetish baobabs, full-moon ceremonies, and the happy or unhappy ghosts for which Kilifi, like Takaungu, Vipingo, Mtwapa, Shimoni and the other Kenyan creeks, was renowned.

In the not-too-distant past, Arabs still sailed to East Africa to fill their dhows with ivory and game skins, spices, coconuts and slaves. Before loading them at night with the high tide, they would chain them to the walls of the ocean caves along the fiords that abound along the Kenyan shores, safe mooring for sailing boats, out of the reach of the ocean's swell.

The spirits of the slaves linger around the many Muslim cemeteries for which the coast is well known, and amid the ancient, mouldy ruins of abandoned towns to be discovered in the forest, among the roots of giant bread-trees and baobabs, overgrown with luscious vegetation, liana and wild orchids. The local people, the Giriama, still kept alive their witchcraft and secret rituals.

I liked all these legends, as they belonged to the atmosphere of mystery and exoticism of the coast, the strange ripe scents of wild jasmine and frangipani, cloves and cinnamon, vanilla and incense, sandalwood and musk; the unusual rich taste of caramelized pineapple, star-fruit, *madafu* and sharp lime; the prevalence of a thousand dangerous snakes and large iguanas, prehistoric monsters with eyes like glass beads, and flickering tongues; the innumerable coloured birds and monkeys, fruit-bats and bushbabies; the solemn baobabs, like columns of vanished temples, and the palms and casuarinas forever shivering with the salty breath of the monsoon.

I had known him for as long as we had been going to Kilifi. Yet although in Paolo's and Emanuele's days we saw much of him whenever we went to the coast, he was really a social acquaintance who had always retained a certain aloofness, and I could not say that, although I liked him, I had known him well.

I was therefore slightly surprised when, in the obscure days after the disappearance of Emanuele, a very sensitive letter of condolence was followed by the message that he would come and visit me in Laikipia for a week.

Emanuele had been dead only three months or so, and the pain of his absence still lingered, shrouding me in waves of solitude and longing.

I had been suffering from a sinus problem, created by the dust, and when he arrived I was still nursing a searing headache. He looked at me and, with half a smile, he dug into his pocket and produced a strange object which he swung in front of my eyes. It was a cone of brass, polished to a bright shine, that had been tied to a length of fishing line. I must have looked puzzled.

'Do you know what this is?' he asked. 'A pendulum. It can be used for a variety of purposes. Particularly to heal, but also to find something that you have lost; to get an answer to a problem; and to discover water. I can try to help you. Then perhaps I shall teach you to dowse with it.'

I was intrigued.

He held his pendulum above my head with firm hands, and sure enough, in a few instants it began to swing, slowly at first, then faster and faster, almost disappearing in a rapid swirl. Just watching it I felt dizzy: then the pain in my forehead seemed to be lifting. In a few minutes I felt much better. I was genuinely amazed.

He suggested that we should try it a few more times over the next day or two, and after that I was totally cured.

'I wish I could do the same. It must be wonderful to be able to help people in such a natural way.'

'You probably could,' he told me seriously. 'Most of us have this capacity, if we would only care to develop it. In the meantime let's go and look for water. We shall see.'

I was at that time trying to occupy myself with the works of the ranch and farm, and needed to locate some places at which to dig bore-holes. His unexpected help was most welcome. As a farmer, he was very knowledgeable about crops and cattle, and was extremely interested in our activities at Ol Ari Nyiro. There was a calm and a depth about him, and it was fascinating to go round the ranch with him, identifying the best locations for a bore-hole.

We would leave the car and set off on foot until we reached a spot that seemed suitable. There we held the pendulum in front of us without moving, waiting for it to rotate or swing on its own. Often nothing happened, but sometimes the reaction was so strong that I was taken by surprise. In this case we double-tested the spot with a rod cut out from a shrub. The first time that it began to vibrate, almost jumping from my hands, and then to point forcefully towards the ground, I was caught completely unawares and was so elated that I almost dropped it. It felt like stepping into a different world, where the unknown forces of the earth that had guided past generations revealed themselves, in their uncanny natural strength and at the same time in all their simplicity.

I was an enthusiastic pupil. Time flew, and I was sorry when the day came for my friend to leave. Just before getting into his car, he took the pendulum from his pocket.

'I would like you to keep this,' he said looking at me seriously. 'But you must promise that you will use it. You have this power, and it is your duty to practise it.'

I protested. I knew how much that pendulum meant to him and I could see that a sort of personal and intimate tie existed between the two of them, rather like that of a wizard and his magic wand, or a witch and her black cat. But he put it firmly into my hands, and, before I knew it, he was gone.

I used the pendulum now and again as time went by, mostly on Sveva when she was sick, and once or twice on my mother and some of my friends. Many felt a certain relief, and I could never work out how large a part suggestion played in this exercise. Most people who knew him remarked how extraordinary it was that he had given me the pendulum, as it was well known how much he valued it. I felt proud to have been chosen.

I did not see much of him over the next few years. I never went down to Kilifi again, as it held too many memories of happy days, and I knew he came to Nairobi only occasionally.

One morning, I sat at my hairdresser in Muthaiga, and was reading a book I had just bought, because the title had triggered my curiosity: *Mysteries*, by Colin Wilson. The first chapter was called 'Ghosts, Ghouls and Pendulums'. Inevitably, I thought of him, and wondered how he was.

We had heard that he had remarried; it had been years since I had seen him.

It was a sudden sensation of being watched, and I lifted my eyes. There, amongst the ladies in curlers and the bottles of shampoos, in the mirror in front of me, I saw him. At the same time he turned his head, our eyes met and he smiled in recognition. I was so astonished by what I could not call a coincidence, that for a moment I could not talk. Instead, I help up my open book towards him, so that he could read what I was reading. His smile simply widened but without a fraction of surprise, as if what had happened had been totally normal.

'With you it was to be expected,' he said calmly. 'Are you well? How is the pendulum?' I noticed he looked tired, almost breathless. It was a hot day.

Only a few weeks later at a dinner party in the Belgian Embassy, someone mentioned casually: 'How tragic, what happened in Kilifi.'

And this is how I heard. He had left his house one morning, with his shotgun, and went off to Takaungu for a walk. He never came back. They had found his headless body in the afternoon, the gun close by, on the stretch of beach along the creek not far from Denys Finch-Hatton's old house.

Nobody could explain what really had happened.

He had gone, this loyal friend of past days, with his mysteries and his stories, a secret pain never to be known. Another Kenyan drama, another ghost to join the ones of Kilifi under the baobab trees.

When I went home I looked for the pendulum, but I could not find it where I had left it. I searched everywhere, for days, combing the house and all possible hiding places. The pendulum seemed to have vanished.

It was only recently that I met his widow for the first time: a good-looking lady who could still not believe what had happened. She wanted to write a book about her life and hoped I could help her with publishers' addresses. She knew I had known her husband, but no more.

At one stage in our conversation, I could not resist asking her about his passion for the pendulum. I was about to tell her that he had given it to me, that I had been very honoured, and that I was now shocked because I could not find it, when suddenly she said:

'About his pendulum. I threw it into the Indian Ocean. It was the only right thing to do.'

The beach, again, was left only to seagulls.

A BED LIKE A VESSEL

Give me the life I love
Bed in the bush with stars to see.

Robert Louis Stevenson,
Songs of Travel, I, 'The Vagabond'

Even if, in the West, we no longer normally believe in the truth of auguries, they are part of Africa and of its traditions. I have chosen Africa, and have grown to accept and to respect its rituals and beliefs, as they are rooted in the very nature of its people and in their simple lives, still close to the source of all things. They are, in their essence, indistinguishable from the instincts which allow tribes to survive in harsh conditions, or migrate periodically to other grazing lands, and which protect them from predators, or guide them to water.

There have been occasions in my life when I have been especially close to the depth of the African spirit, and have felt, with humbleness and pride, that Africa has accepted and, in its inscrutable way, has chosen me too.

Like the time when the Pokot women came to offer me a special wish.

It was the afternoon before Christmas Eve in 1983, when Paolo had been dead three years, Emanuele had followed him a few months before, sent to the country beyond by a snake which could not know what it had done; Sveva, our baby, was about three years old. I was in the kitchen, preparing some complicated chocolate log with my cook Simon.

Rachel, the Nandi maid, had come to call me: '*Kuja! wanawake ya Pokot iko hapa. Unataka kuona wewe.*' 'Come! The Pokot women are here. They want to see you.'

I wiped my hands on a cloth, took my baby on my hip, and went out, licking the chocolate from my fingers.

I could see them all from the verandah, some already squatting, at ease below the fever trees, some standing, some dancing round like long-limbed ostriches lifting their legs high. There were old women, covered in soft skins, their hair in dark greased ringlets, toothless, their craggy lined faces worn like ancient wooden masks. There were the girls, and it was they who sang. They were so young, so frail, like birds who have not grown feathers: stick-like legs, thin arms, gleaming with brass bracelets, and their little round faces on pert necks, plastered startlingly with a mixture of white ashes and chalk in ugly patterns. But their merry eyes, glinting with mischief and teasing anticipation, denied the very purpose of their disguise. They each held a long ceremonial stick which they had gone to cut for themselves from some special shrub in the forest; they oscillated them now in rhythm with their voices.

They sang; and when they saw me, their song gained strength, momentum, as if a sudden wind had given it new wings. It was a shrill, high-pitched lament which sounded like the call of a bird at noon. It ran through them like a shiver as they sang in turn, rippling them into a frenzied, yet curiously composed ritual dance.

It was the song of the girls who have been circumcised, and have borne the pain and the ordeal of this barbaric but accepted tradition with courage and dignity, knowing that they were now free to enter in their role of mature women, and to allow a man to find them, and pay their bride-price of cattle and goats to their fathers. It was the song of the women of Africa, a song of courage and mutual solidarity, of hope of children and proud resignation to an unchosen, yet time-proven fate.

They spat on their hands before shaking them with me

one by one. They giggled, shyly. Some seemed so pitifully small, still almost children, the white of their eyes and teeth standing out in their tribal camouflage, intended to make them repellent to men for the duration of their recovery. In a few days, healed and ready to be seen by all eager young males, they would wear their traditional costumes of bright orange, brown and yellow beads. Their round cheeks would be greased provocatively in red ochre, their hair dressed in complicated tresses, their little breasts bare. Their skirts of beaded calfskin long in the back and gathered in front would reveal their agile legs, tinkling with anklets.

From now on, in the years to come, I would recognize some of them, surprised at the turn of a track, while they tended their goats and weaners, their stomachs bulging with their first and second and subsequent children, year after year, for all their fertile lives.

Suddenly that day, when all the greetings had been exchanged, my symbolic offering of tea and sugar had been passed on, and the ceremony seemed to be drawing to its end, one old woman came forward, proffering in her hands a long object. An instant hush descended on the small crowd like a last layer of leaves after a sudden storm subsides.

All the other women gathered and surrounded me in suspended silence, their faces alert in anticipation. I understood that this was really the major purpose of their visit, and the core of this ceremony. Murmuring guttural words in Pokot, the old woman offered me her gift. It was a wide belt of soft skin, smeared with greased ochre and goat fat, and beaded in a simple pattern with small grey money-cowries like shiny pebbles. Before I knew it, with endearing giggles, they fastened it around my waist, and asked me something I could not understand, with a happy, pressing, even demanding note in their voices.

'*Nyumba yako ya kulala. Hawa nataka kubeba wewe kwa*

kitanda yako.' 'Your bedroom. They want to carry you to your bed,' Simon interpreted for me, appearing at my side like a protecting shadow.

My bed. I remembered the day when I had sat on the floor of the room which would be our bedroom, watching Langat and his assistant Nguare carrying in the trees that would become our bed.

Building a bed is like building a vessel to carry us through the delights and nightmares, surprises and follies, pauses to rest and deliriums of fever during the varied travels of our nocturnal life. Our bed is the most important piece of furniture we may ever use, for so much happens in it to influence our waking hours. A bed is a *habitaculum*, a home in itself. Our sleeping body entrusted to its protection gathers with abandon the strength, the glory of tomorrow's daylight.

Our bed was a four-poster that I had imagined and built of simple and irregular, but polished posts, linked by smaller beams and with a sensational head and foot made from offcuts shorn of their bark, to reveal the sinuous curves of their long woody muscles. This bed, where I still sleep and will for as long as I live, was shaped in a few days inside the room. Tall, massive and unique, it can never be moved out through the small door.

We built it together, Langat, Nguare and I, and when it was ready, I gave them a beer, to celebrate that receptacle of dreams and sorrows. We stood together, admiringly, contemplating the result of our work, and turned to each other to shake hands on it, grinning with the pleasure of recognizing our achievement. The trails that insects had carved laboriously in the surface of the wood created a subtle, inimitable filigree, a delicate fossil memory.

One day – I was then yet to know – Paolo would climb on to the bed and hang from its central beam an empty ostrich egg, to puzzle my soul with the unrevealed oracle he had concealed inside it. I would spend sleepless nights watching that egg after Paolo died, while his baby daughter would nurse and play on the hyrax cover. A few years later, I would lay there, for his last night on earth, the tortured teenage body of my son Emanuele, and I would spend the wake, curled up on my side of the bed, rolled into cold blankets, writing for him my last song.

Show the Pokot women to my bed? The request was so odd and unexpected that I had no time to demur. With a nod, I indicated the way, and amongst cries of triumph, I was suddenly lifted high, above those heads in ringlets, by dozens of strong, skinny hands grasping me tenaciously through my khaki clothes, while a new song was being sung.

They carried me, snaking their way in circles through the garden in a live brown stream, like a procession of harvester ants carrying a large white insect to their secret pantries; before I knew it, my room was full of them, swarming at once and all together.

I was finally thrown, as gently as possible but still roughly enough, on to my bed, amidst howls and giggles from the youngest women, while the older ones proclaimed in a half singsong their prophecy, or their wish. One by one, they all fell silent, until only the oldest one spoke. Hovering over me, searching my eyes with her shining gaze, in guttural bursts she pronounced her sentence. They all chorused the last word, clapped their hands and, one after the other, spat on me their blessing in convulsive sprays of fine spittle. Then I was brought up and out again, dazzled, smeared with ochre, to see the sun.

They explained to me eventually that theirs was a special wish for me, that I should again be happy on that bed which had seen such sorrow – happy, and loved, 'but no more pregnant': the best wish they had to offer, which I accepted gratefully.

And some while after, like all authentic spells, it came true.

12

THE RHINO THAT RAN
FAST ENOUGH

And the experience has left me in some doubt whether a
rhino has such poor sight as it is commonly believed.

Vivienne de Watteville, *Speak to the Earth*

It is often difficult, in Africa, to surprise animals in the
open, as the lush vegetation or thick shrubs provide a
myriad of hiding places, into which the wild creatures,
alarmed by the noise of an approaching car, the crack of a
twig under clumsy feet, or a whiff of your smell carried by a
change of wind, can quickly dive and disappear.

Often have I caught, out of the corner of my eye, a furtive
movement at a bend in the track, the shape of a tail or
flickering ears in the tall grass, and a shadow has dashed away
faster than my mind could register it, leaving an impression,
only, of the passage of some elusive life that challenged my
imagination. Yet, if I stopped to search, scanning the sand or
the dried mud of the game trail, I would find the unmistakable imprint of a large hoof or of a paw, like a signature
unwillingly left by fugitive feet.

The element of chance involved in crossing a path at the
very same moment as a rare or shy animal, and of seeing it
for an instant still in the sunshine or trapped in the car's
headlights, before the savannah grass or the night swallows
it, has never failed to puzzle me. A few seconds earlier, or
later, and the scene would have been missed forever.

I can recall countless such episodes, but perhaps the most

extraordinary of all was an amazing encounter, witnessed with the same sense of wonder by four pairs of eyes. It resulted, through its perfect timing, in the fortuitous rescue of a very rare little creature in distress.

One July morning in Laikipia, when Sveva was about five years old, I drove her down to Centre to fetch her young friend Andrew, Colin and Rocky Francombe's son, to come and play in our house at Kuti.

The air was still and hot, and the sky hung close, the colour of lead, as it is during the season of the rains, when the Highland winds stop blowing for a time, and the only movements are the tremulous flights of white butterflies, migrating westward in endless clouds of palpitating wings. They go, like waves, incessantly in the same direction, as to a rendezvous they cannot miss at the far end of the horizon. The golden air seems full of the snowflakes of an improbable summer storm, or of petals from a creamy bougainvillea scattered in gusts by an invisible breeze.

The transformation the rains brought to Laikipia was always breathtaking. My car skidded in the fresh red mud. The tufts of new grass at the sides of the track were emerald green, and clusters of frothy flowers covered the *carissa* shrubs, mixing their intoxicating jasmine scent with the sweet and warm perfume of the flowering acacias. The wild animals seemed to be reborn, well fed, glowing with health – frisky impala, shiny waterbuck, fat zebra and placid elephant foraging unhurriedly from the taller branches. The red dust which had been dulling the bush like clinging rust had vanished, leaving shining grass leaves and fresh buds. With the children chatting in the back, I was driving slowly back to Kuti, concentrating on the beauty and bounty of the wet, sumptous African landscape.

It happened so suddenly; I was so unprepared. A small grey something darted across the road, almost running straight into the car; a strange little creature like a cut-out cartoon, invading by some trick of imagination the real world around us.

It was a baby rhino, no taller than a dog, dashing in front of me with amazing speed. Alone. Its eyes were fixed on the track ahead, but on perceiving my car they turned towards it and, for a fraction of a second, I could read in them, with great surprise, a look of pure terror. For whatever reason, the baby rhino was scared to death, and I realized that he was running for his life.

He passed inches from my bumper, and in a moment he was gone. I slammed on my brakes, and the car came to a halt, skidding. In the very same instant, another car, coming from the opposite direction, stopped in front of me. In Karanja the driver's face, I read the same astonishment. We looked at each other, and I jumped out of my car to see.

There, standing in the middle of the track, a few metres behind my car, was the smallest black rhino I had ever seen. His skin looked soft and smooth, like a rubber toy. On his nose only an insignificant protuberance indicated where his horn would one day grow. His eyes were tiny, porky, and concentrated on me or, rather, on my car. Absurdly, but surely, I caught in them the reflection of my own surprise, which had wiped off what had been his expression just seconds before: unmistakable, overwhelming terror. And then a definite look of relief, oddly of recognition, of joy almost, flooded into his piggy eyes, as if the encounter had in some weird way comforted him.

An instant later, quite unexpectedly, he began running towards us, aiming straight for my open car door. I did not move, but suddenly my scent was brought to his sensitive nose by a change in the breeze, and human scent meant danger. Startled, looking betrayed, he came to a sudden halt. His head went down, a snort came through tiny nostrils, a comic determination born of instinct took over. He charged and, before I knew it, he knocked his embryonic horn against my bumper. It was so funny that I burst out laughing, and so did the children, whose bewildered faces, with mouths opened in amazement and round eyes which had missed nothing, were pressed to the back window. The noise startled the rhino; and in one movement he turned on his heels, swerved suddenly and trotted off faster than ever through the undergrowth.

Only the bush was left and the empty road, where a faint cloud of dust soon settled.

I turned to Karanja, my other witness, to comment on the event: his mouth, too, was agape, and his eyes widened incredulously. There was more to it than had met my eye. He had been driving a tall land-cruiser and, as the scope of his vision was much wider than mine, he had seen what I could not. His fat hand came out gesticulating excitedly and indicated a point on the side of the road I could not see. I noticed that he had difficulty in finding his voice.

'Simba!!' he screamed at me finally. 'Lion!'

'Iko simba uko nafuata hio mutoto ya faru.' 'There is a lion there following that rhino child.'

That explained the desperate fear. I turned, stood on my tiptoes, and sure enough, through the tall grass and low carissa shrubs, I distinguished the yellow shape of a stalking animal. A moment, and it was gone, leaving the tracks of its claws embedded in the hard soil.

The rhino had disappeared too. His hour had not come yet. Our presence at that precise point in the road at that very moment, had, by some arcane design of fate, saved his life, just in the nick of time. I wondered for how long the chase had been going on. Where was his mother?

Karanja had the answer: 'It is the rhino child whose mother was killed by poachers.'

Why had he run towards me? I thought about it for weeks, and asked all the animal experts I came across for an explanation. Surely he did not come to me to protect him. He was a wild rhino who was not accustomed to humans. But I had been driving a low off-white Subaru, splattered with mud.

Its size, its colour and its shape were familiar to him.

My car was the closest thing to his mother the rhino child had ever seen.

13

FIFTY GUINEAS' PIKE

The seamed hills became black shadows . . . sounds ceased, forms vanished – and the reality of the universe alone remained – a marvellous thing of darkness and glimmers.

Joseph Conrad, *Tales of Unrest*, 'Karain: A Memory'

'Next full moon, I would like to show you and Sveva Fifty Guineas' Pike,' said my friend Hugh Cole. 'The sun will set and the moon will rise, and we will watch from the most fantastic kopje. The view is terrific. Pack some sandwiches. I'll bring the fishing rods. Yeah.'

He grinned. I found his Antipodean accent quite funny for a Cole.

I liked Hugh Cole. He was a true friend of mine, since the old days in Laikipia. The Coles lived, then, on Narok Estate, a large and efficient ranch situated east of us at Ol Ari Nyiro and, by Kenyan standards, they were our neighbours. Often Hugh and our friend Jeremy Block appeared with the specific aim of going after a buffalo with Paolo. They would be out all afternoon, and in the evening we would sit talking until late round the fire.

Hugh was not much older than a boy then – perhaps nineteen or so – and he had dreams, like boys have, and grown-ups too, sometimes.

He was tall and lanky, with straight, dark hair inherited from his Irish ancestors, pale skin with some freckles, and a strange, veiled, deep voice. His most peculiar characteristic was the dancing look of mischief that crept into his disturbing

74

blue eyes, which never blinked and focused on his interlocutor with the disconcerting fixity of a bird. Yet he was much too polite and far too well bred to stare.

Hugh had the flair for words of the June-born. His stories had colour and force, a cutting poignancy which I found entertaining, and in our long talks lay the core of our friendship.

Like the sons of the Delameres, of the Longs and of the Powys families, and of a few others, Hugh had been brought up to farm one day the vast family estates on the Kenya Highlands. They were families who belonged to Kenyan history, and to that earlier generation of eccentric, adventurous or aristocratic Kenyan pioneers who had walked their way through Africa against all odds at the beginning of the century, defying disease and heat, wild animals and tsetse flies, unvisited country and unfriendly tribes. Driven by the invincible curiosity to discover the unknown, they followed the dream of adventure and the need to explore intrinsic to the British soul, and they found a new Eden in the Highlands and on the plains of the Great Rift Valley, where they established their dominion.

They went everywhere on horseback, carving tracks and roads over virgin unwelcoming land. They died of malaria, of mysterious tropical diseases, of septic wounds and festering sores, of native spears or predator's attack. But they cleared the bush and tilled the fields. They bred prize sheep and pedigree cattle, and they shot the lions or rustlers that tried to kill or steal their livestock. They tamed rivers and harnessed springs, irrigated barren land, and planted wheat and maize in hundreds of thousands of acres. Born within the boundaries, imbued with tradition, of a sheltered Victorian upbringing, they were in fact a tough lot.

Despite his inheritance, Hugh Cole's father in time decided to sell Narok to the new Kenyan settlers, as many people in the Laikipia Highlands did.

One day he gave Hugh some money and a pat on the back and he said to him, more or less, as Hugh himself years later narrated: 'Good luck to you, my son. Go safely. You are a Cole. You'll make your fortune.'

Slightly bewildered, Hugh set off to Australia and New Zealand. So did the English conquer the world in days past. But those days were gone, and it was hard for Hugh to find a place for himself in the new continent.

During a visit to America to meet his friend Jeremy Block, another exile, studying at a university, Hugh was involved in a horrific accident. On the bend of a mountain road in Colorado, his powerful motorbike flew off the cliff and while Jeremy, who was on the back seat, remained untouched and shattered only his watch, Hugh fractured most of the bones, big and small, in his body, and almost died.

In Kenya we heard about it, and were desperately worried for him. His recovery took years, and he never quite walked as before. But one day the phone rang and it was my friend Tubby, Jeremy's father.

'Guess who's back!' he said cheerfully. 'Hugh Cole. He is staying with me. Come to dinner.'

Much had happened to me in those intervening years. Paolo had died and my son too. But Laikipia was there in all its immense beauty, and Sveva my new angel, my child of hope and new beginning.

Although he limped and seemed to have grown slightly deaf, he was the same old Hugh, with his chivalrous manners and his well-told stories with outrageous twists; but there was a weariness about him, a new sadness, and of course the amusing hint of a New Zealand accent. He had done a bit of everything down under. Now he was back to see if there was anything more left for him to do here. He came to live with his sister nearby, and I saw him often, having picked up the threads of our friendship. We chatted, we laughed, we spoke of the old days, of people I had lost and he had cared for. My wounds were still open.

The invitation to explore was tempting, and the promise of adventure always holds for me an irresistible appeal. I was curious about Fifty Guineas' Pike. So, on the given day, Hugh came up to Laikipia, in the bouncy green pick-up he used to drive like a maniac, in the back of which he always carried a couple of heavy cement bags to steady it. Sveva – who was then four years old – and I jumped in with a basket of sandwiches, and off we went. At Centre we gave a lift to Mirimuk, the head of our security guards, who wanted to visit some of his Turkana relatives over at Narok Estate.

Hugh had not been back since it had been sold, and of course he still remembered all the short cuts and the best ways through the old *bomas*, every detail of the place where he had grown up. He managed to keep a poker face and to show no emotion while we passed through the land for which he felt, I knew, such an attachment and which had been the background to so many of the stories he had told me; and I admired him for it.

We flew over pot-holes and rocks, biting the dust without mercy, as Hugh had always done. There was about him a new recklessness which was difficult to pin-point. I had no idea where we were going, and it seemed to me at times that even Hugh was no longer sure of his destination.

The landscapes we crossed were breathtaking. Undulating, green hills and open *mbogani* covered in low filigreed *acacia mellifera, sanseveria* and euphorbia. The country was much drier and more desert-like than Ol Ari Nyiro. It took longer than I had expected, hours of rough tracks and bounces, but when we arrived, the place was magical.

One of many kopjes which punctuated the landscape, it probably owed its unusual name to an obscure bet, the nature of which is lost to memory. Fifty Guineas' Pike was sensational and well worth the long journey.

At its foot there was a large pond with a waterfall rolling into it, surrounded by palms and immense, sheer, basalt boulders hung with wild flowers and papyrus. There were tracks of baboons everywhere and leopard spoor. Fish darted about in the pond, large silver barbel, looking like the classic images of fish that a child would draw. Water birds. Dragonflies.

We climbed up the kopje partly pushing and partly carrying Sveva, to the first platform which could be seen from below. There we found ourselves on a flat surface of smooth rock, dotted with deep cylindrical pot-holes, a geological curiosity possibly formed over thousands of years by the erosion of disappeared currents and swirling stones. From here the Ndoto mountains and the North Frontier on one side, and the vast expanse of the entire Laikipia plateau, up to Mount Kenya on the other, stretched as far as the eye could see.

Peering into one of the pot-holes, most of which held a brackish puddle at the bottom, Sveva discovered a small green grass snake, swimming weakly. It must have fallen in when searching for water, and was unable to climb out. We decided to sacrifice one of the fishing rods that Hugh had cut from a long thin branch, and which was rough enough for the small snake to wriggle up. We lowered it at an angle, and, after circling it a couple of times, the snake started slowly winding its way up – to the sun and life and freedom.

'To Emanuele.' Sveva's small voice gave words to my thoughts.

'For Emanuele,' Hugh and I repeated.

The memory of my boy's lost laughter echoed again among the tall grey boulders. He had loved green grass snakes.

It was soon apparent that Sveva, with her short round legs, would be unable to climb the section of large rocks that led

16. The pool at Maji ya Nyoka

17. Kuki and camel

18. Sveva riding camels in the Amaya Valley

19. Osman with the female camel and baby

20. Borau tells his adventure

21. Emanuele in the snake pit at Kuti

22. Emanuele and a spitting cobra

23. Emanuele and a large python

24. Going away. Emanuele's last photograph

25. Sveva at the graves

26. Sveva and Wanjiru

27. Sveva on her 8th birthday

28. Lake Tanganyika: approaching the Mahali Mountains' camp

29. Emanuele at Magic Cove

up to the flat stone platform, which was Hugh's goal, and offered hardly a grip even to us.

The sun was completing its arc in the sky. Nocturnal noises were beginning to creep in among the sounds of daylight. Hugh therefore decided to climb down and drive round to the back of the Pike, from where the ascent was easier. We drove back along our tracks, and at some stage left the beaten path, cutting across the bush for quite a while, heading in the Pike's direction. We parked the car in a small clearing next to a grove of acacia. Hugh took a water bottle and, leaving the parking lights on, we set off on foot.

The sun was fast approaching a chain of hills. Soon it would be dark and we had to hurry. Trusting Hugh's knowledge of the place I did not think to memorize any landmark. The dry yellow grass was tall, the terrain sandy, fairly even, with scattered bushes. Not easy to find tracks here.

We followed narrow game paths, trying to keep up with him in the tall thorny vegetation which did not allow any view, and along corridors of spiky shrubs, winding their way slightly uphill, silhouetted black against the sky. Finally, we reached the back of the Pike and climbed it.

The view was spectacular. Magnificent horizons of craters, kopjes and hills, fading in the pale blues and pinks of the sunset, ran out to the foot of Mount Kenya, its peak covered in clouds, from which the full moon was about to rise. It was announced by the silver lining of the clouds and a pearly luminescence at the rim of the horizon.

Behind us the sun was setting beyond the mountains. Overhead, however, clouds were gathering fast to obliterate the sky and hide the rising moon.

The wind dropped. The clouds were here to stay. We groaned in disappointment. Still hoping the sky would clear, we chatted, drank some water, sang a song. Suddenly it was pitch dark.

It was soon apparent that the moon would not become visible for hours tonight. Baboons began to bark their goodnights from the sleeping cliffs; alarmed goodnights, for rather close we heard the unmistakable, rhythmic, rasping voice of leopard. If I had been alone, I would not have hesitated and would have slept there, safe on the flat warm rock. But Sveva was tired and would be hungry, and it could easily rain.

We descended from the platform by the way we had come, tentatively now, Sveva gripping my shoulders, and we landed in the thick bush. We then tried to find our way back to the car, and it was a mistake. I had a pocket torch, but its tiny light, absorbing and distorting every shape, made the encircling night darker, vaster and confusing. Every bush of *mellifera* looked like every other, hung with powdery yellow flowers unendingly identical. Every next turn of the sandy game path seemed like the last one. The hills were now invisible, and with no reference we walked fatally in circles.

Finally Hugh cleared his throat and turned to me. I heard his deep disembodied voice spell out from the shadows what so far we had not dared to admit.

'My friend, I am afraid I have got you lost. I am sorry.'

At the word 'lost' Sveva wailed.

I had never been lost before. I was surprised how unsettling and undignified the very thought was. Ideas came racing through my mind and failed to find solutions. I became impatient and angry in my dismay. The anger was mostly annoyance with myself, at my stupidity. I should have found out more, looked around better and not allowed such a ridiculous and unnecessary situation to happen. Getting lost indeed. I took hold of myself.

'You brought us here, and you are going to get us out of here.' I coolly told a crestfallen Hugh, trying to convey in my voice a calm and flippancy I was far from feeling.

Sveva's hands clutched my shoulder:

'I want Wanjiru,' she declared with a hint of defiance in her trembling voice. 'And the *askari* and my room. And I want Morby.' Morby was her beloved soft pink mouse. She must have felt immensely remote from her safe known world, hanging from my back, lost in the African night. I tried to reassure her:

'We shall find the right track any moment. It is great fun to be here. No little girl we know was ever as lucky as you are. Imagine, a real adventure to tell your friends. Now you must help me to guess where to go. In the meantime, we shall find a cosy place to wait.'

Many times, while looking for lost cattle in thick bush and rocky terrain, with no visibility even in daylight, I had seen Luka, our tracker in the old days, smell the wind as he followed a track he could not see, turning his head here and there and going off in an unlikely direction which was infallibly the right one. I had been curious to know how he could do this, and often asked him to tell me how he managed. He had looked at me in puzzlement, for following an instinct is something impossible to explain. Invariably he had said: '*Lazima jaribu kufikiria kama nyama, memshaab. Ngombe hapa wataenda kulia kufuata arufu ya maji – hama kutoroka arufu ya simba.*' 'Try to think like an animal, memsaab. Here a steer would now go right, towards the smell of water, or away from the smell of lion. Cannot you see?'

So I tried to think like an animal, which meant following my instinct, without resorting to my reason at all. It told me to turn and go in a certain direction. Shortsighted and in the dark, God knows how I could. I prayed we would not meet a buffalo coming to water.

We advanced tentatively, often to find thorns tugging at our clothes, pulling our hair and scratching our bare legs. I tried hard to see the bright side of things. At least it was not pouring with rain; at least it was quite warm, and the air was balmy with heady scents. It was a beautiful night, after all. I was in Africa where I had always wanted to be and this was a mysterious place, undisturbed by people. This *was* the quintessential adventure. At every turn of the narrow track I strained my ears to anticipate a grunt too close, a rustle of leaves.

Amazingly, a white and wider track suddenly opened in front of us, and with unspeakable relief I realized it was the road. But at which point on it? And where was the car – right or left?

The only wise decision was for Sveva and me to stay right here, with our back to a large shrub for protection, to light a fire to discourage nosy beasts, and to wait. Hugh would go on looking for the car. If by sunrise he had not returned, I would set out on my own to find the car tracks. There was no sensible alternative. Staying where we were was safer than wandering about with a small child in the darkness near a watering hole. I was certain that all sorts of animals would come to drink there in the night; I remembered the spoor we had seen.

We gathered some sticks and larger branches by the light of my little torch which was beginning to glimmer only tremulously now, and Hugh lit a fire with a dexterity learned in the free days of his childhood. The orange flames leapt high, crackling, and the shadows receded to a wavering circle with borders of mystery from which countless eyes seemed to peer at us.

The fire lifted my spirit, and Sveva lay on my khaki sweater, quiet now, and listening, like I was.

Hugh stood a moment and took his neck scarf off.

'I shall tie this to a bush at the point where I leave the road.' He grinned once. 'Are you sure you will be all right?'

He bowed slightly and was gone.

Around our small fire, and its warm halo of light, like a dot in the universe, the night was black and vast and alive with unknown, magnified noises. Red and brown ticks sidled away fast from the flames, running diagonally like minute crabs. I kept telling Sveva stories, without a pause, to cover the yelling laughter of the hyena, and the threatening voices of the invisible and of the unknown. I sat with my child out in the African night, which for once did not belong to us, feeding the fire with thorny branches of *mellifera*, and trying not to think, or rather planning what to do, if the lion which we heard roaring from the hills decided to come to drink at Fifty Guineas' Pike. My ears strained to catch all whispers, to interpret secret shuffles, a sudden roar that froze my throat for a moment, trotting of heavy hooves along dry paths.

My Italian past was far away that night. Yet there was a primal beauty and privilege in being here as we were: where was the rest of the world?

With the infallible knowledge of a child born and brought up in the bush, Sveva broke the silence now and again.

'Mummy, hyena.' Something had yelled.

Or, on a close trumpeting: 'Elephant!'

Something coughed: 'A leopard!'

A burst of loud, untidy barks: '. . . and he is eating a baboon, Mummy.'

She was probably right. African noises can tell their story far more eloquently than human words.

Looking at the fire and nursing it, time ticked by with the ancient sound of crackling embers until, my watch forgotten, my head lost in thought, a peace descended, and the awareness of being safe. A total calm and the feeling of being in the right place.

Gradually, and then abruptly, the great clouds parted like waves, and in a crystal clear sky a cool full moon sailed silent and aloof above, ignoring us. It was hard to believe that this was the same moon people were watching at this same time from a London window or a Venetian gondola. The unknown hills were clear-cut against a translucent sky, and a deafening concert of crickets and frogs erupted to greet the moon. The nearby sounds were friendly, and soon became a concert of which we, too, were a part. There was a silvery magic about the place and us, alone and vulnerable, yet accepted by the creatures of the night. I let the fire quieten down, twinkling, subdued and no longer needed.

I took Sveva in my arms, her warmth and child's fragrance comforting and safe. I knew well that I would never again capture the essence of Africa as I had tonight. Time went by. I was happy. And it was with regret, not relief, that much later I heard the muffled hum of an approaching engine and car lights put an end to the spell.

We laughed with abandon, like reckless children. I covered the glowing cinders with sand and got into the car, but as the sun began to rise and the familiar shapes of the Laikipia hills came into focus, we grew silent. Sveva was sleeping, and the adventure receded like all dreams at dawn, to become a memory.

14

THE COBRA WHO CAME
FROM THE DARK

Todo dejò de ser, menos tus ojos.*

Pablo Neruda,
Cien Sonetos de Amor, Noche XC

The feeling lingers of a drifting young presence below the shadows of the yellow fever trees in the night garden. A voice comes sometimes with the voice of the wind, joining the starlings' song in the full moon and the crystal calls of the tree-frogs from the fishpond. A faint voice, like the echo of my memories, and the unreachable essence of dreams.

It is then, when I am alone in the heart of my home, protected by my dogs sleeping content around me on the carpet, the fire's flame subsiding into breathing, flickering embers, that he comes back. In the quiet room, behind my desk, there is suddenly a presence. I do not turn my head. I keep watching the enlargement of the photograph hung on the wall, the one taken by Oria after that last picnic at the springs.

Forever he goes away up my wall, leaning forward, in the red dust of his motorbike, driving fast toward the hills, without turning his head to look back.

I search, sometimes, when I walk alone in the sunsets, for his lost voice, for phrases already spoken and forever gone. I recall how he walked, how he shook his head to clear away the hair from his forehead or a thought from his mind. But the image comes and goes away too quickly, dissolving before

* 'I could see nothing more, apart from your eyes.'

85

I can quite manage to grasp it and savour it, before I can fix it in the hourglass of my present. I cannot smell any longer the warm smell of his young boy's skin toasted by the sun, and it is only the scent of buffalo and elephant, of jasmine and sage, which mixes with the breeze from the east, blending with the sound of birds and the rustle of alarmed gazelles and jumping hares.

What remain forever of him, are only his eyes.

From the drifting fog of my vision only his head seemed to emerge; his mouth curved slowly in a spreading luminous smile, and the firm unwavering eyes kept looking inside me unblinkingly, yet without staring. The background seemed to take on an intense, unearthly nuance of vivid blue, vibrant with a cosmic quality which I perceived, but could not explain. A smooth shape, with glistening marbled skin and beady, lustrous eyes, coiled easily just below his chin.

I stirred.

'I can see him. He seems serene. He looks peaceful. And he is serious. Strange. He . . . has a snake around his neck.'

The lady in the red sari smiled. Her short white hair was cut like a man's, but a lock touched the red dot of paint forming a fine upward pointing arrow in the middle of her forehead. The eyes glowed bright like burning coals and they transmitted care and warmth, mixed with the unusual gift of a totally accepted and mastered insight. She put her hand on mine, and instant heat radiated from the dry palm. Her brown fingers, adorned with silver and gold rings, rested a moment on mine, and I felt a surge of great peace, an encompassing calm overtaking me. I closed my eyes and, even before she spoke, I knew that what she was going to say would be the answer to so many of my questions, and that it would be right. The weird, uncanny tie between Emanuele and whatever was Indian.

'Breathe deeply. Yes, Kuki. But to finish his karma just do

what I tell you, when you return to Kenya. It does not matter if you believe it or not; one does so many things without knowing why. It will not hurt to do it. With Sveva, the first night you are back.'

Outside the tall window, the great mountain peaked with snow, whose shape seemed to me inexplicably familiar, hovered benign and extremely powerful. I had heard that some people found it threatening, and oppressive, and fled from it in fear. To me it was a protecting strength, fully deserving its old Red Indian name 'The Mother'.

The shadows of a setting, late-summer, American sun advanced slowly, and the granite boulders of the summit were suddenly tinged a deep blood red. For the first time I understood the reason for their name, Sangre de Cristo Mountains. And their blood was my own, and everyone's, the sadness of the universe, and Emanuele's blood.

The milk filled the cup. Sveva withdrew the jug she was holding and looked up at me.

'I think it is enough. Let us go.'

We went out into the darkening garden, followed by our patient dogs. It was another sunset, short and of drifting blues and reds and greys.

Our guests had retired for an evening shower and to change for dinner.

Sveva and I were alone, and this was the right time.

At the end of the garden the fire the *askari* had just lit was gaining strength, and its light, blending with the fading glow of the setting sun, was not yet in contrast with the darkening night.

The dogs ran ahead, chasing each other, and looking back curiously at the wooden bowl Sveva was holding. Together we managed to fix it, without spilling a drop, in the fork of Emanuele's tree, so that the dogs could not reach the milk.

We stood side by side as we had been told, murmuring together the words that the Indian priestess had taught us, the haunting Hindu sing-song of the Vedic mantra. Strange, soothing words we could not understand.

Their sound, their purpose, suddenly struck me as being of the same essence as any Christian, Muslim or Jewish prayer, or any pagan invocation, the instinct of humans to try and reach out to touch the inexplicable infinite that we call God. Their unknown meaning, by rendering them arcane, magic, and in a way more plausible, matched the incomprehensible mystery of death. For different reasons, in different languages, but with similar rituals, millions of people were praying, at that very time, with the same hope to the same Unknown to whom they gave different names. Standing on the Highlands of Kenya in the gathering darkness, the Latin murmurs in the churches of my childhood were closer to me than they had been in a lifetime.

Om's echo drifted away, floating between the wings of the wandering nocturnal plovers, whose voices sent a rain of arrows to the sky. The fire burned fiercely, fed by the wind. I touched both trunks in a lingering caress; the soft yellow fluff of the fever trees planted on Emanuele and Paolo's graves trapped the warmth of the sun like a human body.

Sveva and I walked back, holding hands. In the fishpond a half-moon was reflected. But amongst the papyrus, where the little silvery tree-frogs hide, inflating their small throats like pearly bubbles in a trilling song of bells, there was no movement. We searched the still oily water with our torch, but we could see no goldfish gliding away lazily below the waterlilies, under the carpet of salvinia. The fishpond seemed strangely silent that night.

We went back to the house, where another fire had been lit on the fireplace.

Early next morning, devoured by curiosity, still with our

nightgowns under our caftans, Sveva and I went to look. Nothing seemed to have changed in the night. Even from a distance, we could see the wooden bowl lodged in the same place, between the arms of the smaller fever tree. I took Sveva on my hip, so that she too could look at the same time. Small sugar ants busily climbed through the fluffy bark. Up in the intertwined branches filtering the morning sun, a starling perched, and flew off. We looked, holding our breath.

The bowl was empty.

We walked back in total silence, not daring to give words to our thoughts which had no answers. Sveva threw a piece of her morning toast into the fish pond. A normal action. The bread disturbed the floating weeds, ripple after ripple unbalanced the blue water hyacinths, but no fish or frogs dashed up from the bottom to grab the food. The bread remained uneaten. All life seemed to have abandoned the fish pond. It was puzzling. I went to look for one of the gardeners to ask if any ibis or stork had come to eat the fish.

The one *shamba* boy I found had not seen any.

It was dark when we came back that night, after a long game drive with the car full of guests and friends. We were commenting on the troupe of baboons always perched on the tallest trees at Marati Ine, just above a rotten trunk where Emanuele had found his first cobra. The gardeners were waiting at the outside gate. I stopped the car to ask what was the matter.

'*Bunduki.*' 'A gun,' said Francis. 'We wanted to ask permission to call a watchman with a gun to shoot the snake.'

A feeling of hair rising at the nape of my neck. A feeling of having looked down into the unknown, to discover a familiar, yet indecipherable link.

I switched the engine off while everyone was listening.

'Which snake?'

'The one who came last night. We saw him at the graves, but he disappeared into the fish pond.'

That explained the eerie silence.

'Which type of snake?'

I found it difficult to find my voice. Sheelah had told us which. The snake sacred to Shiva, the most deadly, the most holy of all.

'*Kiko*,' said Francis. A cobra. Then his voice lowered to an awestruck murmur:

'But we have never seen the like of him around here. He is the large variety. The one which stands straight upright.'

The giant forest cobra. The king of cobras. The most holy of all.

'Mamma!' Sveva was shouting in the waiting silence. 'Sheela had told you. We must let her know. It worked. The mantra worked. Emanuele is all right now.'

'No gun,' was all I said to the gardeners. 'Leave that snake alone. As he has come, so he will go, and he will follow his ways and the ones of his spirit god.'

Next morning we went to the fish pond, Sveva and I. Weaver birds were flying in and out, busily ripping the papyrus into shreds for their nests. Midges flew in a small cloud and dragonflies darted jerkily from a creamy waterlily to a blue one. When Sveva threw in her bread, dozens of fishes of all sizes sprang to life from the muddy bottom, fighting for the bobbing morsels.

The cobra had gone. The soul could rest.

15

ELEPHANT BALLAD

For HRH Prince Bernhard of The Netherlands

Recognizing that a creature of another species is in danger
from one's own kind; going to the aid of that creature . . .
imply the exercise of true compassion and also other most
sensitive emotions.

Ivan T. Sanderson: *The Dynasty of Abu: A History and
Natural History of Elephant and their Relatives, Past and
Present*

Its breath is said to be a cure for headaches in man.

Cassiodorus, *Variae*, X, 30

The man limped towards my car holding on to rudimentary crutches made of cut branches. Below his loose turban, feverish eyes peered at me above gaunt cheeks.

'*Jambo!*' he addressed me shakily. '*Mimi ni ile ulikufa mwaka hi. Unakumbuka mimi? Ulitembelea musijana yako na ngamia.*' 'I am the one who has died this year. Do you still know me? I used to bring your young girl riding with my camels.'

Of course I remembered him. His name was Borau, a camel handler of the Boran tribe, whom we had employed in Laikipia for years. He herded camels day after day, and often came up to Kuti to hold the bridle of Sveva's camel when, at four or five, she had developed a passion for camel riding. He spoke constantly to his camels in the ancient camel language developed over generations and generations of close relationship with these extraordinary creatures, the noblest of African livestock and essential to the survival of his tribe and the related Somalis.

'*Toh-toh galla.*' The camel sat, crashing down on its knees.

'*Oh. Ohohoh oh galla.*' And the camel went.

'*Ahiaeh ellahereh.*' And the camel drank.

'*Kir-kir-kir.*' The camel trotted faster and faster . . . and so on.

Day after day, off went Borau at sunrise to guide his herd to the grazing grounds. Until one day he met the elephant.

A morning like all September mornings; a sky of deep rose and the stillness of dawn; the profile of the horizon black, with sculpted acacia trees; birds chattering from the *lelechwa* shrubs; and a yellow sun, round and flaming, rising in a glow of promised heat.

The camels had waited patiently, chewing their cud with a crusty noise of long worn teeth, sitting on knobbly knees, and surveying through sad eyelashes the morning preparations in the *boma*. A hot mug of spiced tea to wash away sleep; a bowl of sour camel milk; incitations, calls, and they were on their way. His camel stick firm across his shoulders, today Borau headed towards Marati Mbili.

He liked his job. He knew nothing else but walking in front of the camels, timing his agile step to their rhythm, curiously similar to them in his long ambling steps and his thin legs with heavy joints, built to march without pause. Or walking behind the camels, following their large soft feet that raised no dust, and left only neat rounded prints, like the shadows of a leaf.

He knew their favourite browse, and interpreted their needs like all herdsmen who match their lives to those of the animals they tend. His very existence was camels.

Today was drinking day for the camels, and Borau decided to wash in the *marati*. The camels drank first, extending their necks to the troughs, stimulated by the Song of Water, a triumphant biblical lament as ancient as the need to drink.

'*Hayee helleree, oho helleheree.*'

Immediately after drinking, the camels started grazing,

nibbling with prehensile lips on nearby bushes and filling their discerning mouths with *carissa* leaves. The sun was higher now, and Borau slid off his *shuka* and his head-scarf to wash.

It was then that a big young male camel, who had been mauled by lion, started a courting skirmish with one of the females, but was intercepted instantly by the dominant rutting male. The old camel came behind the suitor with frightening gurgles, and chased him off furiously. The younger one crashed away through the bushes with alarming speed, and was instantly lost to sight.

It is extraordinary how suddenly and completely the African bush can swallow animals. A shiver runs through the leaves, as the shrubs recompose themselves like ripples settling after a plunging stone. A cloud of dust suspended in the air; a whiff of rank smell; a sudden intake of our breath; perhaps the impression of a shadow, darting too quickly to let us focus on what we think we have seen. Only the prints of feet running on the track remain to prove that a herd of animals has just passed.

Borau sped after his camel, dressing while he ran. He tracked its rounded foot marks, but soon lost them in a mess of fresh elephant prints round a muddy water-hole. He looked and looked in vain; not only did the abundant elephant spoor confuse any other marks, but it announced the presence of a large invisible herd. It was wiser to go back to the camels, and make sure they did not become frightened and scatter in all directions.

Now, from the signs he saw, he knew the elephants were ahead of him. Not that it mattered. Borau was used to this. He just ought to be on guard, make sure he remained downwind, so that his scent would not alarm them, and move on light feet, hardly touching the soil, like the impala.

Soon he sighted the backsides of two elephants emerging

from the sage just a few steps in front of him. He moved behind them carefully, all his senses alert so as not to disturb them.

He never heard the cow elephant which followed silently. He never saw her, until it was too late.

An instinctive glance over his shoulder. A large hovering shadow obscuring the sun for an instant, the pungent smell of ripe dung and hay, a hot breath fanning his neck and shoulders. The look of a yellow eye fixed on him, from a few feet above. Large grey ears flattened against grey temples. Extended trunk curled up to expose long tusks. The horrible recognition that the elephant was after him, and that he could not escape.

Blind terror squeezed his heart and Borau ran.

In total silence, the elephant ran after him. She was a heavily pregnant female, young enough to be quick, agile, and gain deadly speed; old enough to remember that man is the only danger to elephant. Old enough also to have been part of a group caught in a poaching ambush, when the screams of pain and the smell of the blood of her fallen companions left an indelible mark in her memory. And female elephants are known to become overprotective, often touchy and aggressive in the time immediately before and after they give birth.

Borau ran and ran, mindless of thorns and sticks tearing his clothes apart, blinded by the sweat filling his eyes, and while he ran, he knew that he was going to die.

The thought of a slender girl, her velvet eyes laughing below her head-shawl; a bowl of camel milk steaming in the chill of dawn; the call of a child running towards him; the familiar hollow sound of the wooden camel bell. The simple things of his lost life now beyond his reach.

The earth vibrated, shaken by the elephant's feet, and by the thumping noise of his heart.

He wildly looked around for somewhere to hide, for a tree to climb. But there are no trees, in thick *lelechwa* country. Then the impenetrable, impassable *lelechwa* gave way to an open *mbogani*, littered with roots and boughs. One caught his foot, and he tripped, face down, on to the hardened soil, his nose squashed into the dust. With a jerk he turned and looked up.

The elephant was on him.

In perfect silence she went down on her knees at his side, and in one movement lifted her tusks high and plunged them down into his leg. The tusks were butter-coloured but hard as spears, and like spears they penetrated his thigh like butter. The snap of fractured bone sounded like the snap of a broken branch. No pain. A spreading numbness.

The elephant stood, towering over him, looking down at his squirming body, as if to make sure he could hurt her no more. Slowly, deliberately, she lifted her foot above him. He screamed.

Startled by the strange noise, she stiffened, her foot hesitated and, in this pause, Borau instantly saw his chance and started pleading. If his camels understood, why not the elephant.

'*Hapana. Hapana, ndovu. Wacha. Kwenda. Akuue mimi, tafadhali akuue rafiki yako.*' 'No. No, elephant. Leave me. Go. Do not kill me, please do not kill your friend.'

Had the elephant cow ever heard a human voice before? The new sound pierced her opened ears, puzzling them with a new note. She seemed to listen. Her large ears flapped once, twice. Her foot came down on to the exposed face, but not to hurt. It stopped almost in mid-air, then descended to touch him.

Borau was too shocked to protect his face with his hands, and the elephant's nail caught his turban, and undid it. The material came loose, covering his eyes. The foot hovered over him slowly, delicately, brushing down the length of his whimpering body, but pausing to feel his head and chest. He could see now the furrows dug into the sole of the elephant foot by walking thousand and thousand miles over thorns and rocks. She probed him with surprising gentleness, as if the sound of pain and fear in his moaning voice was one she could understand.

After a while she stood back, and, more confident now, Borau agitated his hands and began calling out loud with all his remaining strength, the camel's command to run: '*Kir-kir, kir-kir.*' Go fast. Go fast. He screamed louder and louder.

The elephant shook her head from side to side a few times, as if to chase that sound away stamping round him in the dust. Then she turned, and crashed away trumpeting. Only the cicadas remained, to fill the sudden silence with their eager songs.

The pain began to pulsate. Borau's mouth was parched and dry, his leg wet with blood and urine. He tried to move, to crawl towards the direction of the track, but he could not.

Perhaps the people back at the camp would notice that he was missing; when night came they would come and look for him and find him. But when night came so would the hyenas, and the lion, and the little silver-back jackals with their greedy mouths. If a sheep or a steer were lost, he knew it would never survive a night outside the *boma*.

The smell of blood, the smell of fear would attract all the scavengers. It was strange that there were no vultures yet; only the formidable presence of the elephant could have discouraged them, but he knew they would not be long in coming. In Africa there was always a vulture circling high, close to the sun, looking down with its telescopic eye for a dying animal on the plains.

The vultures would come from the sky, free-falling fast like bombs, and land on a branch, gathering their wings about them – first one, then another and another, until all the trees around would be black with them. While the air filled with the sinister sounds of their presence, the vultures would sit and wait with undertakers' patience, and they would not have to wait long. Then one would come close, with awkward leaps, flapping his wings with raucous chortles of anticipation – the grotesque vulture that goes for the eyes first.

Visions of death and carnage filled Borau's mind – a sense of his own total vulnerability, crushed, unable to move, dying alone in the bush, an easy prey to any animal of the African night. He wondered at his own destiny, he who so many times had escaped malaria and the grip of high fevers, and infections and wild animals. Was it the wish of Allah that his road had reached its end in such a way?

The sun was setting now, he knew by the changed sounds of the bush; the sun he saluted every morning and to which he prayed every night. He tried to talk to Allah. Was God too remote from this *lelechwa* country?

He prayed for company, for any company. And he soon realized that God had listened.

He was not alone.

Slowly, through the fog of his total misery, Borau became aware of presences round him. They were gathering quietly, betrayed only by a noise of a broken branch, by a stomach gurgle, a shuffle, a deep breath, a rustle of leaves. They were extraordinarily quiet, and they were coming towards him. Their large feet did not hammer the ground. They waded through the bush with great ease and the calm of creatures who are unafraid. Soon their vast grey shapes cast vast shadows over him.

And Borau knew, without fear, that the herd of elephant had come back.

Earlier they had stopped feeding to watch what was happening. Now they came curious and unfrightened, to see what it was, this small trembling animal on the ground. First, came the young ones, tended by the matriarchs; they ran to him with open ears and stopped a few feet away, to observe him with attentive eyes. Then, one by one, the entire herd approached until they all stood round him, watching.

With feverish eyes, Borau looked up at the elephants as they looked down at him. He gazed into their yellow eyes, which examined him with benevolent attention, and he could feel that they would not harm him. In a weird way, he knew that, on the contrary, they would shelter him from the nocturnal dangers, and that for as long as they were there to guard him, no predator would dare to approach.

For a very long time, they stood in silence, as if studying him, and during that time, Borau talked to them. Heads lowered towards him, ears wide open, while they appeared to listen to the universal language of pain and surrender.

A trunk lifted, stretched, reached out and then another, Tentatively, smelling him and feeling him as gently as the caring hand of a nursing friend, they all touched him with their trunks. Quietly, they inspected him, carefully, unhurriedly, as if to reassure him.

Night had now fallen, with calls of guinea-fowl, grass-crickets, tree-frogs and nightjars. The elephant began to feed around him, like silent guardians. Now and again they each came back to stroke him. They ate, and then they came and checked, as if to reassure themselves that he was still there and fine, as if to reassure him that they were there to protect him.

Time drew on; Borau curled up on the cool spiky grass, trembling now with fever and shock, almost unconscious, but feeling utterly safe in their mighty protection.

They waited there around him while night approached. And who knows for how long they might have stayed. Even when the sound of an engine broke the silence, they still waited, alert now, with heads held high to smell the wind, ready to flee from the only animal of which they were scared. Car lights pierced the night and human voices; the engine droned closer now, advancing wheels opening up the shrubs.

Only then, like a school of dolphins going back to their ocean, leaving the shipwrecked sailor they have brought ashore to the care of a rescuing boat, did the elephants disappear, noiselessly, into the dark.

16

AIDAN'S RETURN

I am waiting for a welcome sound, the tinkling of his camel bell.
                    Isobel Burton, Letter to Lady Paget

The magic of the Highlands of East Africa is the evenings, when the noises and the colours and the very essence of the air change, and a wind begins to blow in sudden blasts, bringing with it tales of places far away.

It is then that we can imagine anything may happen, and while the sun takes on a light of deep red before setting, all the memories, all the prayers, and all the tears we have ever shed flock around us, squeezing our hearts with often unbearable pain.

I walked out facing the wind, all my dogs running ahead, in a flurry of tails and joyous barking. I walked up the airstrip at Kuti towards the green hills where euphorbias grow thick, and watched a herd of elephant slowly moving through the bush, towards the water-tank hidden by trees.

The dogs took off, all at once, after a gigantic male warthog, their fierce barking swallowed by the growing shadows. I found an old anthill, big enough to sit upon, and crouched there, gathering my shawl about me, my feet on a twisted *mutamayo* bleached by age, to write my diary. Harvester ants hurried down their hole, carrying the last yellow seeds of the day. In the crepuscular sky, huge clouds shone, of the deepest coral. The hill of Mugongo ya Ngurue looked black in the twilight.

So often, over the years, this had been my familiar evening

walk. Alone; sometimes with Sveva; in the recent past with Robin, and his hair had been the colour of the bleached grass at sunrise, his laughter fresh, sincere and a balm on my wounds. Since our paths had gently parted as it was written, the dogs were my only companions, and my deep longing for Aidan, the man who had eluded me.

A couple of years after Paolo's death, and a secluded, lonely life filled only by the presence of my children – Emanuele, then a teenager, and Sveva, who had been born after Paolo's fatal accident – destiny had one day guided me to a country wedding, and there I had met him for the first time.

Tall in the crowd stood my love, and I recognized him. In his strange, secret way he recognized me too. For a time we shared the music of my sheltered room, we knew our faces by candlelight, and the smells were of incense, of love, and cut flowers in vases.

What I knew more about him was the intent look of his stirring blue eyes, the deep voice in the poems he read to me, the feeling of his strong, demanding body, his arm outstretched from the window of his white car in the grey light of early morning.

I gave him all I could, but the time was not ripe yet. He had to go, leaving me waiting, at the bottom of my solitude, but taking with him the key to my door, just as he held tight, already and for ever, in his long fine hands, the key to my inner self.

Of Aidan I missed the masculine presence, the deep voice and the searching eyes, the subtle poetry and inexplicable appeal of the solitary nomad, the adventurous man who walked alone and to whom the wild was familiar. Aidan had no fear in the bush. His confidence came from his knowledge and love of things untamed, of plants unknown and of paths not yet trodden by human feet.

I missed him with a longing to which I could give no name. With a patience which was most uncharacteristic of me, and with unreasonable faith, I waited for years for the time when he would be back. Evening after evening, when I was in Laikipia, I walked up this airstrip with only one hope. If the power of my yearning could be a magnet, I knew that he would be drawn back. When the time was right, I would be ready.

I listened to the noises that every African night always brings: guinea-fowl and nightjars, a far whine of hyena, a faint mooing of cattle being herded to an invisible *boma* behind Kuti hill. The elephant, the largest, were as ever the quietest of all. Only a broken branch and a stomach rumble betrayed their closeness. On the horizon a white sliver of moon began to rise.

I waited quietly, with a sense of encompassing peace, for the friendly darkness. My dogs, now back, formed a protecting circle of warm panting bodies round me. Silence. From the top of the termite hill, I could watch with no fear.

The sound came suddenly from behind the treetops, in a still pearly sky. It was like the distant buzz of a persistent insect, approaching fast and growing louder in the stillness of dusk. I knew instantly what it was and at the same time I saw it. A small white aeroplane approached from the east, suspended in the sky, flying low over the trees, gliding over the hills, and straight towards me.

It was too late for a small plane to fly. In a few minutes it would be dark; nowhere could a small plane land over the shady precipices and valleys of the Great Rift, unless . . .

I stood slowly, and all the dogs with me.

The wind, again, took away the noise and there it was, circling over Kuti hill, pointing towards Nagirir, lower, much lower, white wings outstretched like a bird flying home. Before I could gather my thoughts, and calm the surging emotions and the wild thumping of my throat, here it was, landing in a cloud of dust.

I walked uncertain to the centre of the strip, my back to the silver moon. In the last glimmer of dusk the plane glinted, turned towards me and came to a stop. Shading my eyes, my heart just pounding, I moved slowly towards it, unbelieving. I had dreamed for years that this might one day happen.

A few weeks before, there had been a letter, inserted in a musty old book, a rare first edition of an autobiographical novel by his favourite uncle. So enthralling was the story, and so masterly the passionate style of writing, that the book had been haunting me since, as had the note – the first in years – with its elusive promise.

'I often talk to you, who are sitting on my shoulder. Things have changed. One of these evenings I will come to find you. If you would ever . . .'

Now there he was, as ever unexpected, landing for the first time on the strip I had built for him in past days of misery, as only happens in those tales in books.

Even before the tall shadow jumped out, I was running. I stopped a few steps away. He had changed little: a slender living statue with broad shoulders, searching eyes in the serious sunburnt face, straight nose, tight curly hair, firm soft lips. He moved a step. I moved a step. We moved together, and he caught me, crushing me against his breast without a word.

'I'll never leave you again,' he whispered on my mouth.

So came back Aidan.

17

UPON THE WINGS OF THE WIND

In memory of Tim Ward-Booth

Yea, he did fly upon the wings of the wind.
Psalms XVIII, 10

L ife in Kenya, with its extraordinary beauty and variety of opportunities, its unbounded space and spectacular landscapes teeming with wild animals, its lakes and deserts, mountain ranges and countless beaches, its savannah, forests and windswept Highlands, attracts people of an unusual quality, who regard risk and challenge as an intrinsic part of the *safari* of existence. They fly with the moonlight and land in the dark; they hunt alone for lion and buffalo in thick bush, or for crocodile, wading waist-deep into rivers and lakes; alone they climb deceiving mountains; they explore on foot waterless deserts and forbidding country where bandits are known to attack travellers; they dive in shark-infested waters, or sail with light craft in turbulent seas; they defy malaria, yellow fever and tropical disease; they approach dangerous animals to study or film them. They gaily court danger, and, although a number of them perish, quite a few manage to survive.

But for too many, as for some who live more conventional lives, the end of the adventure is simply a road and a lorry which does not stop.

Kenya's tarmac roads are notoriously unsafe, populated as they are by unworthy vehicles and irresponsible drivers, who race at full speed careless of rules, leaving chaos and tragedy in their wake. Among them the worst by far is the Mombasa road, where hundreds die every year in terrible accidents, the majority of which could have been avoided. So died Paolo, and dozens of people I have known. One of them was Tim.

When I think of Tim, now that his time on earth has gone, and his body rests on a hilltop overlooking the desert of Kenya's Northern Frontier, as close to the sky as when he lived, what I remember most is the beat of his last helicopter, and that of my first. It was an afternoon years ago, soon after we had met, when he flew me down through the shadows of the Mukutan gorge.

The deafening noise of a helicopter's propeller always reminds me of a struggling gigantic insect flapping its wings in a last frantic attempt to fly. Over that noise his voice sounded clear and deep.

'Are you ready?'

He turned towards me, grinning. I noticed the curls on his straight head, the handsome and masculine features, the Roman nose, reminiscent of Paolo's. Like all men who fly, his eyes had a different quality – penetrating and yet at peace, shining with the innocence and cleanness of the space over the prairies of clouds, infinitely remote from the polluted world of the crawling creatures below.

There was this aura about Tim that I had only sensed before in men I remembered long after the echo of their steps had faded down the corridors of time. Men who did not live for long, whom I could not imagine growing old. It was a presence both warm and aloof, strong yet gentle, which commanded instant respect. He did not talk much. He moved straight, with no effort of his long lean legs, his skin tanned golden by the Equator's sun.

I looked out of the convex glass window, at the sheer cliffs of rock hung with aloes and thorny euphorbias, and down at the dense carpet of palm tops and fig trees which covers the bottom of the Mukutan gorge. For years I had wanted to explore the depths of the canyon, which are impenetrable to humans, fit only for eagles, vultures and daring helicopters of silver.

The occasion was during the period, soon after Emanuele's death, when Robin had come into my life. He was working on a film about a jungle adventure which involved a scene with a helicopter, to be shot at Nyahururu, formerly Thomson's Falls, about forty miles from Ol Ari Nyiro. Tim was the helicopter pilot. I went to visit the set, and in the evening I invited Tim to spend the night in Laikipia with Robin and me, and to fly us down the Mukutan gorge. He was quick to agree, and we went.

I was ready and nodded. My heart beat hard in my head, and there was a rush of heat to my face, as we began to plunge into a vertical dive, encapsulated in that precarious metallic machine which sounded so much like a crazed dragonfly. I looked at the back of Robin's head. He was in the front seat. His neck hardened in tension, a rivulet of sweat trickling down into his blue shirt.

The gradients of rugged rocks were so precipitous, so mercilessly steep that only Tim's skill, refined in the time when he had served in the Falklands war, could carry us through the narrow passages. But I had suddenly no fear at all. He was totally at one with his machine, poised and completely in charge, as balanced and light and precise as the bird perched on a slight swaying treetop I had once watched with wonder in the Seychelles.

Tim concentrated on the command panel, his ancient profile still and timeless like the portraits of warriors engraved on Roman coins. His eyes narrowed, and we were dropping along the sheer walls of pink and grey stone towards the tufts of the treetops 3,000 feet below. I felt the same mixture of elation and worry, of being physically winded and mentally exhilarated that I had as a child, on my first wild swoop down the highest, steepest slide at the Luna Park.

The green leaves were suddenly too close, almost touching the keel. For a few moments we were tentatively brushing the treetops, like a bird searching for a safe branch to perch on. Then we glided horizontally along the narrow bottom of the valley, past waterfalls, tangles of liana and dracaena, monkeys and eagles and quiet unvisited ponds. Soon we were surging again up high, to the top of the canyon, where boulders of granite had for millennia guarded the silence and mysteries known only to the African creatures. There we emerged into the different windswept world of the Highlands plateau, the vast limitless expanse of the ridges of Jaila ya Nugu, Nagirir, Kurmakini, Mlima ya Kissu and the familiar favourite promontory of Mugongo ya Ngurue.

The sun was swallowed by the valley, and the shadows spread fast on the hills. We had veered obliquely towards my house at Kuti, low over the bushes, scattering some outraged elephants, while buffalo looked up, rooted on their stocky legs, more puzzled than aggressive for once.

We landed on my lawn. The staff and all the dogs had gathered together in a bewildered group to watch in awe, from a distance, the flying object from another star descending in the dusk. They clapped their hands and jumped up and down and laughed on discovering that it was Robin and me who disembarked, running, our hair windblown, with Tim following. And he was laughing too.

Years later came the afternoon at Lewa Downs. This time I stood at Aidan's side. Tim had been his cousin. The scene was unreal, the beauty and the pathos of Africa were at their most dramatic.

In the haze of noon, one after the other, cars of all descriptions drove up the hill. They parked in neat lines, just below the four army helicopters which rested incongruously on the grassy slope. People got out in silence, and climbed up to the summit, where half a dozen armed African rangers in khaki-green uniforms stood to attention, a depth of sadness in their still features. The women's skirts and hair moved in the light wind. In the pure sky, unblemished by clouds, a solitary vulture flew, close to the sun.

A few giraffe ambled quietly to the shade of a yellow fever tree down in the valley, and to the north the views of pale lilac hills stretched ahead unendingly to the distant horizon.

From a four-wheel-drive car emerged a girl, dressed in black. She had been driving back to Nairobi on the Mombasa road and there she had found a body thrown into the middle of the tarmac – the killer lorry gone. It had just happened. It was Tim. Courageously she had put him in the back of her car and had driven him straight to the hospital in Nairobi. Only in Africa can such things still happen.

She moved towards the lady, dressed in white, who was his mother. I introduced them and watched in respect while they embraced. The first woman to see him alive, and the last. Encounters at the limit of human experience.

People met like this on that hilltop at Lewa Downs on the afternoon of the burial. People who had come from far for this last goodbye; people who knew each other well; people who had never met; some who would later become friends; others who would never meet again. All of them, tomorrow, would go back once more to their diverse, separate lives.

Then the silence was broken by a strange pulsating sound coming from the sky. I looked up. The vulture had gone, and here, as unexpected to me as the unicorn of legends, was another helicopter.

It landed on the peak. Music started, like a lament. The

doors opened. All the men took off their hats, and his friends approached to take his coffin. They carried it in silence to the very edge of the hill, where they placed it among garlands of heather from the moorlands of Mount Kenya.

Suddenly, with a tremendous noise of flapping wings, almost from nowhere, two more helicopters converged simultaneously on the hilltop, and for endless moments they stayed still, suspended over the valley, facing the coffin and level with it in a glorious salute, while a man in uniform, tears rolling down his cheeks, played the Last Post.

18

THE RING AND THE LAKE

Or speak to the earth, and it shall teach thee.
The Book of Job, XII, 8

There is in Colorado a very special place called The Baca, an immense ranch spreading at the foot of the Sangre de Cristo Mountains, where the air is thin and heady, the sunsets long and deep red, and the light golden and pure as I have only found it before in the Highlands of Kenya.

In the mornings deer come down from the snowy mountain they call The Mother, and you can see them grazing undisturbed, like impala, on the bleached grasslands which remind me of the savannah. The flowers are yellow and blue and have a dry, long-lasting quality. A wild sage, valued by the Red Indians for their ceremonies, grows on the mountain slopes, and its aroma is the same as that of the *lelechwa*, the sage which grows wild in Laikipia on the edge of the Great Rift Valley.

Like Laikipia, from where you can see Baringo, one of the many lakes for which the Rift Valley is famous, The Baca opens up into the great Saint Louis Valley, which was once upon a time an immense lake, now sunken out of view. You can still sense there the proximity of water in the smell of the wind, in the vegetation – pines and cactus and herbs of an almost Mediterranean quality, in the parched sandy terrain which reminds you of the shores of an African lake, and in the astonishing miracle of the Great Sand Dunes, a small ever-changing Sahara of breathtaking beauty, whose shivering patterns are like those left by the waves of a receding tide.

11. Paolo and Emanuele perched on an old dead tree
on the edge of the Great Rift Valley

12. Emanuele with green grass snakes

13. Sveva on Leppy

14. (*above*) Night at Ol Ari Nyiro Springs: Sveva and Leah
15. (*opposite above*) Laikipia: with the anti-poaching patrols
16. (*opposite below*) Simon Itot

17. (*above*) Kuki and her dogs welcoming a plane landing at Kuti
during an elephant count

18. (*opposite above*) Sveva carrying a large tusk for the 1989 Ivory Fire

19. (*opposite below*) Kuki and Sveva

20. The nest on the Mukutan: only local materials were used to build it

21. Kuki writing in her nest above the Springs

The place has long been renowned for its spiritual power, and since time immemorial was used by the American Indians of all tribes as a healing ground where, their wars forgotten, they could come to bury their hatchets and worship their gods, dedicating themselves to the sacred ceremonies of their traditions.

It was there that I met Sheelah. She was an Indian priestess of an ancient Vedic sect, one of a number of religious groups who had been welcomed to The Baca by its enlightened new owners, so that the place would continue to be a spiritual retreat on a larger scale, embracing all of the world's old religions. It was a time of soul-searching for me, after the death of my husband and son. With my small daughter Sveva I had accepted the invitation of Maurice Strong and his wife Hanne who, after visiting Laikipia, had seen the extraordinary similarities between the two places. They suggested that I would find at The Baca something which would help to heal my wounds.

'There is a fire ceremony tomorrow morning at seven down by the creek. Come,' said Hanne, the first night we were there.

A fire was lit every night at my graves in Laikipia, at the bottom of my garden. I found fire evocative, purifying and I was intrigued by the idea of a fire ceremony. We went.

We followed a shady path along a stream, beside the gentle murmur of running waters, to a glade where a group was assembled around a large fires built in a pit in the ground. Symbolic offerings of fruit, flowers, rice and honey were assembled on one side, a large shining rock crystal reflected the morning light, and fine incense smoke drifted in the cold, clean air. People were sitting in a circle, and among them, dressed in a red sari, was a small woman.

Instantly I had the odd feeling of having met her before; and when she turned to look straight at me and smiled, I felt I had known her for ever.

'I am Sheelah Devi Singh. Welcome to our fire ceremony.'

Her eyes were brown and simmering with a bright, hot light. She took my hand, and her fingers were hot and dry and burning too. An arrow with a red tip was painted on her forehead, like a flame; the fire cast orange reflections on her olive skin and short cropped white hair; my feeling about Sheelah, from the beginning, was that she was made of the substance of fire.

It was a simple ritual with mantras and ancient songs in Sanskrit, to thank Mother Earth for her gifts, to give her back symbolic offerings and to ask for simple wishes of peace and healing to be bestowed upon us. I found it soothing and timeless, and I gained from it a sensation of lasting harmony, a quiet in my soul. It was right to give back some of what we took. I have learned since, in fact, that what one gives always comes back, often in various forms and different ways.

I saw Sheelah often after this, during subsequent visits to The Baca over the years, and occasionally attended her fire ceremonies in the early mornings. She belonged to the Rajput tribe, the most noble of all, whose warriors ride into battle carrying spears. She had followed her religious calling after an unusual life, and, although my rational and independent mind has never allowed me to adopt a specific faith, nor to give my spiritual search a definite label, I found her philosophy and her music a soothing and positive presence at that time of my life.

A bond older than friendship seemed to grow between us. With her I went through the unforgettable experience of transcendental meditation through deep breathing, which lifted me out of my own body and made me go back into a forgotten past, where images of former lives disclosed themselves to me, and left me with an accomplished feeling of great peace, of total happiness.

Indian beliefs had always fascinated me. Sheelah explained them to me with a mystic simplicity which I found ineffable, and when she sang with her harmonium, the sounds of the unknown words dug in my soul odd echoes of reminiscence.

When Sveva was about to be eight years old, we went to The Baca for a few weeks in the summer. Unknown to us, Sheelah travelled all the way from Bombay, where she now lived, to be there for her birthday. Eight is an auspicious number in Eastern tradition.

Sveva would be eight on the eighteenth day of the eighth month of 1988; we were at 8,000 feet; there were many people, and when we counted them it did not seem like a coincidence that they were eighty-eight. I gave Sveva eight presents, and the last was a magic wand.

Sheelah had brought gifts of old silver, incense and silk, and Hanne had arranged for an old hippie from Boulder to come and play his cymbal to Sveva for good omen. Its vibrations reverberating in the morning air sent shivers down our spines.

At a special fire ceremony for her birthday that morning Sveva, dressed in red, with a flower behind her ear, fair hair streaming down her back, was arrestingly beautiful. She took all this with a serious grace that was exquisitely hers, and I felt that allowing her the opportunity of experiencing, while still so young, many aspects of the human search for the infinite, could only add to her inner growth.

On the day before we left to come back to Africa, Sheelah unexpectedly knelt in front of me and took from her own feet the two gold rings which adorned her middle toes. Without a word she put them on mine. In her brown eyes was a loving warmth mixed with an inscrutable sibylline detachment. Her voice had a singsong accent and an almost hypnotic quality.

'You will wear these as if you were a Rajput, and you will

never lose them. You must have courage. You are my sister, and we shall meet again, perhaps in other lifetimes. You will travel the world, and many people will be around you. You are going to write a book, and the next few years are going to be full of action. You will succeed in your dream through your hard work. It will be up to you, and you will make it. Remember that the choice is always yours. Never give up. You have much to do. Emanuele is at peace now, and Paolo . . .'

She looked at Sveva, who smiled at her and at me with Paolo's eyes.

I wore my rings on my toes always, after that day. When people remarked on them, I told them it was a long story.

I wrote my book, and this kept me away from The Baca for some years. The Gallmann Memorial Foundation grew, and its activities took all my time, all my attention. I wrote at night, like an owl, so as not to steal time from my daily work. I established the education project in Emanuele's memory and I developed many others too in Laikipia. Aidan flew back into my life, to bring passion and adventure. Sveva grew harmoniously, and I felt fulfilled.

I never saw Sheelah again. A few years later I heard that she had died as a result of falling from her horse at The Baca. I felt her loss, but I knew that it was a fit way to move ahead, for a proud Rajput.

The rings became even more precious. Occasionally it happened that one or the other got caught in the grass, or in the thick fabric of a carpet when I was walking barefoot, or among my blankets; but uncannily they were always found again. So much so, that I came really to believe that I could never lose them, and this became a joke among my house staff in Laikipia.

'*Pete yangu ulipotea tena.*' 'I have lost my ring again,' I would tell Julius.

'*Sisi tapata, tu. Wewe awesi kupotea hio pete kamili.*' 'We shall find it. You cannot really lose that ring for good,' he would answer with a smile.

And, sure enough, a few hours later he, or Simon, or Rachel, or one of the gardeners, would appear with my toe-ring in their hand.

Sheelah's rings became a sort of special talisman, and looking at them glinting on my toes I never failed to feel pride, gratitude, and a certain comfort.

Last summer Sveva, Aidan and I flew to Lake Tanganyika. We left the plane on a tiny airstrip cut out of the tropical bush, next to a village, built only with natural materials; plastic, tin and cement had not yet reached the lake shores. It was an amazing place, still belonging to a remote time that so-called civilization had not managed to alter. On a peninsula outside the village we saw, while passing in the boat bound for our camp, a weird scene of witchcraft, as if in an account of Burton's early explorations. Seven dead cats were hanging on shrubs to propitiate the spirits of the water.

Extraordinary trees grew along the lake, and tangles of rare plants to Aidan's delight, and the time was one of bliss, love and sheer happiness.

We stayed in a fantastic camp of white tents, like a sultan's, that stood on a white beach, where we were the only guests. It was a place of pure enchantment. Every day we walked up into the forest to look for elusive chimpanzees. We swam in the cool water and went for sunset expeditions in the boat, fishing in unvisited rivers for small yellow and black fish that appeared surprised to see us.

On the last day we went for a long walk up the mountain, alive with butterflies and strange creepers and liana. It was extremely hot, and after trekking up and down the hills we welcomed the freshness of the lake water, which is as transparent as the most crystal-clear sea. We took off our shoes and our clothes, left them in the spreading shade of a large mango tree, and ran into the lake to swim.

It was while walking back to the camp along the shore, our feet in the waves, that I realized one of my rings was missing. The currents were powerful, with a swell that was curiously similar to the ocean tides. The sand was coarse, with small shells and pebbles, and it sloped steeply down below the water. My feet had sunk into it, and there was no way a small, non-floating object could ever be found again once it had been captured by the sucking waters. It looked as if this time my ring was lost for ever. I felt deeply sad, deprived.

We walked up and down the beach many times, searching in vain amongst the debris for a golden glint: but we knew that there was no point. Turbulent waves continuously swept the shores clean. The proverbial needle in the haystack would have been infinitely easier to find than my toe-ring in the lake. A white depression on my toe marked the ring's place. It would fade in time, as I should not substitute it with another.

I was crestfallen for part of the day, but then, as the shadows grew long, I became resigned to this irreversible loss and understood that it was up to me to accept it, and let go. I decided that I should make a special, positive gift of it to Lake Tanganyika in Sheelah's memory. In her fire ceremony she spoke to the earth and gave it back symbols of what humans thanklessly took: plants, water, scent, minerals. A golden ring was the perfect offering.

At sunset I went with Sveva to the waterside. We both noticed that, in an eerie way, the colours in the sky were the same deep blood red as the Colorado sunsets. We recited ceremonially an almost forgotten mantra that Sheelah had taught us in the old days, the mantra of giving, which ends with '*Swaha*', the word which was pronounced after each offering.

I thought vaguely of the Venetian Doges who every year threw a precious ring into the Lagoon, in a symbolic marriage with the sea.

Now with a light heart I offered to the great lake the ring that it had already taken; with thanks for its beauty and the happiness we had experienced there.

'Lake Tanganyika, I offer you my ring. I am glad that, if it had to go, you took it. *Swaha*.'

I felt somehow relieved after this, as I knew it was the right thing to have done. Hand in hand, I walked with Sveva back to Aidan and our tents.

We had finished packing, the next morning, and the boat was waiting to take us back to the airstrip carved out of the forest. I was in my tent having a last look round before going.

The man came running from the mess tent and stopped a few feet from me.

'*Memsaab*,' he said, '*nafikiri hio ni yako*.' 'I think this is yours.' '*Ulikwa kwa mchanga*.' 'It was on the sand.' He held out something in his hand. It glittered, and in the morning sun it seemed to wink. Behind him, the lake was glimmering, benign and generous, with all its secrets.

With a thumping heart, while Aidan and Sveva watched in total silence, I reached out to take back my ring.

19

THE RAIN-STICK

For Isabella

There was a roaring in the wind all night;
The rain came heavily and fell in floods.

William Wordsworth,
'Resolution and Independence'

The aeroplane came to a halt in a cloud of red dust, roaring its engines while it turned towards us. The girl jumped out, dressed in beige linen, beautiful, still pale from the journey and the strain of an American winter.

'I heard you had a drought,' were her first words, and she held out to me a long object, wrapped in brown paper.

She looked around. On every side of the strip at Kuti, skeletal shrubs and dusty yellow stubs of grass painfully broke the hard crust of murram, mute witnesses to her words. It was the second year of a harsh and painful drought. Thorns and dust were all that was left of the green, vibrant bush.

'Here is my present; it is a rain-stick. I bought it at an American Indian shop in New York. They say it is infallible.' She grinned. Her stunning eyes glinted with gold mischief.

'I hope it works. It looks as if you really need it.'

It was the morning of 24 December, and in my large verandah, below the thatched *makuti* roof, the Christmas tree glittered its unexpected tinsel reflections in a merciless equatorial sun. The air was hot, and still, and dry, with no hope of moisture. The sprinklers turned and turned slowly, tired on my lawn, spraying the flower beds with perfunctory jets of water which were instantly absorbed by the thirsty soil. Birds flew in to shower, shaking and ruffling up their feathers with chirping trills of pleasure; and the go-away birds cried from the treetops their raucous noon calls, querulous as ever.

I did not want to unwrap the rain-stick yet, as it was a Christmas gift, but when I took it in my hands an extraordinary noise of running water came from it, a liquid sound of droplets streaming through its length with a passionate intensity. It sounded like a shower of rain falling on a thatched roof with powerful abundance: a forgotten sound. If anything could attract rain, it was surely this.

When had our last rainfall been? It did seem ages. The worst drought ever was killing Kenya's crops, animals and people. A famine of unrecorded cruelty was ravaging the Northern Frontier, where parched camels' carcasses lay on the sand beside desiccated water-holes in the quivering heat, and people died like ants day after day, of malnutrition and thirst and nameless disease and lost hopes.

It had been a terrible time. Over a period of two years with practically no rain our water-holes had dried out. Islands had emerged from the large dams that had reached their lowest level, and were rimmed with dusty patches of unhealthy green reeds where the water had once been. Algae grew on the surface, suffocating the life below. Clouds of dead tilapia appeared bloated on the surface, poisoning the depths. Our cattle had lost condition and many had to be sold; the remaining animals struggled to survive on a sparse diet of sticks and dust and salt. Buffalo were found dead every day. Skinny gazelles, with sad eyes and unhealthy coats, stood in forlorn groups, licking the dust. Even the mighty elephants looked thin, their ribs showing beneath the corrugated skin, and each night herd after herd persistently attacked my garden, the only oasis of green in a vast area.

The ranch was dying, and there was nothing we could do. It was late December. No rain could be expected before the end of April. But there was no way we could survive until then. We needed a miracle; I could surely do with a rain-stick.

The rain-stick, when I finally gave in to my curiosity, was a simple section of bamboo, thick and decorated with a fringe of red and black silk ribbon. It had been crafted cleverly, with much thought. When I touched it and turned it upside-down an invisible series of seeds fell through it and touched the hidden thorns which perforated its length at intervals, interrupting their fall and resounding like secret castanets; it was an uncanny sound of rain on a roof-top. I brought it in triumph to the kitchen, and explained to the staff its infallible spell. '*Ni miti ya mvua. Natoka ngambo, mbali, kutoka mganga ya asamani. Ni kali sana.*' 'It is a stick to make rain. It comes from far away across the sea, built by old witch doctors. It is very powerful.' With the unquestioning African faith in talismans, they instantly believed me. '*Tasaidia sisi,*' Simon the cook declared seriously, accepting its magic with simplicity. '*Asante sana.*' 'It will help us. Thank you'.

They all nodded wisely and touched, in awe, the occult instrument of rain.

I shook it up in the air with naive emphasis, begging the gods for rain. Rachel and Julius clapped but did not laugh. One does not play with mysteries.

That night, believe it or not, the first tentative drops began falling without much enthusiasm on the tin roof of the bedrooms. January is one of the driest months of the year in Kenya. It was highly unlikely that any rain would fall for months. I woke up at the noise, lit a candle and looked out of my window. A cool wind blew, and with it came a distracted spray of sparse warm drops. I took the rain-stick from my bedside table and shook it a bit more for good measure.

Was it an impression? Did the sound of rain gain momentum? A coincidence? A delusion? It seemed so, for the next day the sun was as blazing hot as ever. But a faint scattering of raindrop marks on the dust of the driveway was proof enough for my staff, who came to ask me if I could please beg again with the rain-stick.

And so it happened. It began surreptitiously: a difference in the wind; masses of dark grey clouds coming from the east, and passing through without stopping, like flocks of foreign sheep in the silent sky. A sound of far-off thunder in the early mornings, and in the evenings a sickly rim of silver on the horizon, blackening the sun. A stillness in the air, a chill suddenly creeping into the hot noons with drifting shadows.

Then the news came that it was raining up north, over the Chalbi desert. On a ranch called Borana several inches fell in one day. People murmured in wonder.

We had arranged to take a few days off, and go to a camp in Samburu, called Kitich, on the Mathews range. The Mathews were dry mountains with forests and ancient cycads, and rivers of great beauty. I flew in with Aidan and Sveva, while Jeremy Block followed with his plane, his father and other friends. The mountains appeared shrouded in clouds, and the closer we approached the more we could smell rain. Even from the air we could see wet patches on the tracks.

When we landed, the strip was so wet that, had it not been sandy, we could never have made it. Jeremy took off again immediately for Colchecchio ranch, which belonged to my old friend Carletto, to ferry in some more friends from there to join the party.

'You'll never make it back, with all this rain!' we joked.

Rain in Colchecchio in January was out of the question. We all laughed, but somehow we all felt a premonition, and as I looked up, the clouds seemed to gather faster, covering in mist the mountain tops. We drove in two packed Land Rovers, slipping through mud, often sliding sideways, and with great difficulty we twice crossed a river which seemed to get fuller by the moment. Our guide shook his head.

'If it goes on raining tonight, the track will be blocked, and we shall never be able to drive back through the river.' He looked confused. 'We have never seen anything like it since I have been here.'

Along the road we met a thin black goat, happily herded by two craggy Samburu elders dressed in red. Red and white glass bead ornaments glinted from their earlobes, like tiny antlers. They wanted a lift, but there was no way two extra people and a goat could be squeezed in with us. The Samburu went on their way, waving goodbyes.

'It is the goat for the leopard,' explained the driver.

We observed it with curiosity. It was really skinny, with a bloated stomach.

'They will slaughter it, and then we shall hang half of it from a tree.' He smiled broadly: 'We shall eat the other half.'

'The leopard is very hungry. He shall surely come tonight to eat it.'

And we would watch the leopard coming to the bait.

We looked at the innocent goat trotting along unknowingly to her fate. Strangely, somehow, there was no real cruelty in the scheme, as the leopard would take a goat each night anyway, and the camp would buy one for the staff stew, and the fact that this one was designated for a sacrifice seemed to fit well with the Samburu's business. They all needed cash after that long nasty drought.

We proceeded so slowly in the mud that by the time we reached the camp we found the two old Samburu there, leaning on their sticks. The unfortunate goat had mercifully been already *chinjad*. Our tents were new and comfortable, near the river bank. The river was full, and to our surprise huge tree trunks were being carried off on its tumultuous waters, proving that unusually heavy rains must have fallen on the forested mountain tops.

It started drizzling soon after we arrived, and by the

afternoon it was raining so hard that we could not leave our tents. Some even had to be moved, as the ever-rising water lapped at the flies of their verandahs. The only dry places were our beds where we repaired for most of the time, and I managed to read again, after years, the entire unlikely story of *The Portrait of Dorian Gray.*

Only Aidan, unworried by the elements as he could be, took off with his rucksack in the rain and came back in the dark, soaking wet, his *kikapu* filled with strange succulent plants.

We crept out in the evening for dinner, giggling at the absurdity of this adventure, and during the first course in the dripping mess tent, our attention was drawn to the lit tree across the river, where half the goat hung from a branch. There was a large genet cat on it, pulling off chunks of meat with hungry determination. We stood watching until suddenly from the dark foliage a shadow jumped up into the tree, the branch swayed, and a leopard crouched in all its mystery in the light, grabbing the carcass with its claws.

The genet cat's mistake was its greed. The leopard, impatient of competition, swerved to one side, and with a casual jerk snapped its fangs on the genet's neck. It trapped the genet in its powerful jaws and shook it twice; we saw a shiver pass through the grey lithe creature, and its limp body was thrown carelessly off the branch, back into the darkness, leaving us breathless. As if nothing had happened, the leopard went back to the goat, to feed on it, indifferent to the heavy rain, until only a few bones were left.

This was the major event of the wettest two days of my life. Jeremy was never able to fly back to join us, because Colchecchio – we heard on the camp's radio that first evening – was under water, with thick fogs, and a constant deluge.

Eventually, we had to leave on foot in the torrential rain, wading through the river with water up to our necks, the luggage balanced perilously on our porters' heads. We walked all the miles back to the aeroplane, which stood on its sandy strip on the hill, glistening with moisture.

We flew back through steamy mists over new swamps and muddy, swirling rivers which filled the *luggas* and inundated the sands around for miles. Five inches of rain had fallen over a day and two nights. Two of Carletto's dam walls had collapsed at Colchecchio, and torrents of water flooded the plains where zebra and giraffe ran bewildered.

The rains had come to Laikipia too. Night after night I lay on my bed listening to the water gushing down the roof. Our big dam filled in a few days. As if by miracle, grass sprouted again on the barren savannah; slowly at first, animals regained condition, and the elephants for a time forgot my garden.

We found that rainstorms had spread through the country, causing unprecedented floods everywhere. Bridges had collapsed, trains had gone off the rails, rivers and lakes overflowed, and panels of experts were puzzled to find answers to this extraordinary change in the weather pattern, unrecorded in human memory. Fantastic new explanations appeared in the newspapers every day. Even the BBC World Service, the Bible of all good Kenyans, spoke about it.

January 1993 was declared the wettest January in the history of Kenya. The final explanation was that a cyclone bound for Madagascar had, for no apparent reason, changed route and poured its avalanches of water on to the parched soil of Kenya. Wherever one went, people exclaimed in surprise.

But we, at Ol Ari Nyiro, knew better. On my bedside table the rain-stick lay enigmatic, and many of the ranch people came over to thank it. With knowing glances, wherever I went on the ranch, they alluded to its powerful medicine. Even the Pokot came to know about it, and they suggested that every season I should go with it where rain seemed to be most needed.

Now it is March, and the dams are again beginning to dry out. People start whispering that I should use the rain-stick once more. But I prefer to wait, as the gods should not be bothered too often. I shall resist and wait to the end of April, when the rains are meant to come anyway. And when the sky begins to darken with clouds from the east, I shall again, with reverence, use the rain-stick from the Red Indians to attract rain to this land once more.

The rain-stick belongs to myths and legends; and as one has learnt in all the tales one has read as a child, magic powers should not be abused, lest one should lose them.

20

BIRTHDAY IN TURKANA

My birthday began with the water-
Birds and the birds of the winged trees flying my name.
Dylan Thomas, 'Poem in October'

When Sveva was about to be ten years old, I asked her:
'Now, tell me. Where would you like to celebrate your tenth birthday? It is a most important one, the first one with two figures.'

She looked at me with those turquoise blue eyes, like Venetian trade beads, which had been Paolo's.

'Choose something special,' I continued, 'a symbol of what you would like to do for the next ten years. And tell me why.'

I did not know what she would ask. But as I knew she had come from a wild seed of unpredictability, I anticipated that it would not be obvious – not a party with cakes and music, pony rides and fancy dresses, confetti, presents for each little friend and perhaps a treasure-hunt.

There was the time – she was about eight years old – soon after our Turkana companion and guide Mirimuk had died, when she asked to spend the night of a half-term out in the bush with me in Laikipia, without a tent. We went alone to Luoniek dam, and, after eating and telling each other stories around a fire of *lelechwa* roots, we had slept on a large mattress on the ground, under a mosquito net tied to a small tree as an illusion of protection.

In the middle of the night a noise woke me up. Grey and massive in the light of the moon, hovering above us so close that he could easily have touched us, was a large male elephant. He had stopped next to us to pee, and was attracted by the net flapping in the breeze. Totally still, head tilted on one side, he seemed to be listening. His tusks stood out, white in the moonlight.

I caught my breath and looked at Sveva. She was fast asleep next to me, curled up in her blanket, her fair hair spread on the pillow, and she appeared innocent and vulnerable, so terribly small below the tall elephant shadow. I moved my head close to hers and murmured in her ear, while squeezing her arm gently:

'Wake up. There is an elephant here. Do not move. Be ready to run into the car when I tell you.'

My Toyota, with the back door open, was parked nearby.

Unlike children normally shaken from deep sleep, she opened her eyes instantly and fixed them into mine, slightly glazed for only a moment. Then, without moving her head at all, she turned them up and considered the elephant. She was not worried by what she saw.

'We'll be fine,' she murmured with a smile; then she closed her eyes and in no time she was asleep again. Soon the elephant moved away quietly. I shall never forget that incident.

Now she considered my question. It did not take her long. She smiled brightly, glowing as ever.

'I would like to go to an island in Lake Turkana, because you said it's wild and beautiful, and Papa Paolo and Emanuele loved it. It will be right to be in a place where I have never been yet, because there will be nobody there, apart from us, and because for the next ten years of my life I want to see special wild places where few people go.'

'That's a deal,' I said happily. It had been ages since I had travelled to Turkana myself.

Turkana of the savage, torrid winds, like the breath of hidden giants; of the basalt rocks and immense waters, and crocodiles and huge fish; of solitude and silence, and spectacular landscapes: I longed to go back. But, to an island? How? There were no islands large enough to have an airstrip, and few real airstrips round the lake apart from one at the oasis of Loyangalani, and another in the north near Ethiopia, at Koobi Fora where Richard Leakey had his anthropological dig. And we had no boat. There was only one island flat enough to land on, and was the remote, deserted South Island.

So strong were the winds and so barren the waterless dunes, that no one lived there. Only untamed Turkana fishermen, naked or clad in the flimsiest loincloth, reached it on fishing *safaris*, after rowing through turbulent, crocodile-infested waters, in their wooden canoes packed with harpoons and hand-made sisal nets.

There was no strip, just an almost flat area, like a curving track through the rocks and rare thorn trees, with a bend and a dip in its middle, as if drawn in the black sand by the swishing tail of a dinosaur.

I had heard about the island's extraordinary beauty, its dramatic landscapes, the difficulty of reaching it, the danger of landing there in high winds. For years I had heard about its bewitching spell.

Among the places I had always wanted to see, but had never found the right person to go with, or the right circumstances, South Island in Turkana was certainly first. But among my friends with an aeroplane, there was not one of whom I would dare to ask such a favour.

So, South Island had remained beyond my reach. As with all places long coveted, the yearning made it more precious, unattainable. As with all places of essential simplicity and stark spiritual quality, I felt the adventure of its discovery should only be shared with someone I felt deeply in tune with.

But now there was one person in my life who could help to make this mad dream come true. Aidan.

He was the one who walked alone, exploring virgin mountains and unvisited deserts. He loved travelling through new country with only his camels and camel handlers for company. He knew the African bush, and he knew the sky.

He flew his small plane with legendary ease and could land anywhere – on a road, on a beach, on the sand, by the light of the moon or of a hurricane lamp.

Our relationship had known the test of time and the agony of separation, but when it pleased the gods he had flown back into my life. I was allowed to see his eyes by daylight, and to walk at his side in the sun: together we could smell dry grasses, dusts and growing things. Now was the time of travelling together to strange places.

There came a week of walking with his camels through deserts, and the bewilderment of the desert kiss. There was the time he flew me for hours over parched hills to a place of antique Muslim dignity and traditional hospitality, a small town on the border of Ethiopia.

There was a day when we landed on a forsaken strip in the middle of nowhere, and walked along a dry river bed to find a biblical well, herds of camels and goats, and wild herders in turbans and loose *shukas*. And there was the night when the noise of a light aircraft landing on my strip at Kuti had woken me up, and I had run out, followed by my dogs, to find him walking up my drive.

'I thought there was just enough moon to ask you for a moonlight walk.' He had smiled at me. Sveva, who had been spending that night in a tent in the garden with a friend for fun and adventure, told me next day they had believed a rocket from another star had landed on our strip.

Aidan was, beyond doubt, the ideal companion for South Island in Turkana. Sveva's tenth birthday was the ideal occasion. My daughter and my man: what a perfect combination.

The aeroplane skidded in the black sand towards a bare hill tinged with orange, and with a last roar the engine stopped. Then there was only the silence of the island, coated with the fire of the evening.

I opened the door and jumped out. The warm wind of

Turkana touched me again, after many years, bringing the soft soda smell, the cry of a crow, and a wave of memories. The wind caught Sveva's hair in a sunny swirl.

'Thank you, Mamma!'

I turned round, shaking my fringe from my eyes, and as far as I could see there was only water, volcanic sands, black gravel, yellow hills, and mountains devoid of any human life. We were the only people on earth, and the first ones, and the last ones.

I squeezed Sveva tight; her head already reached my chin; she would be very tall one day soon.

'Happy birthday, *amore*.'

So, this was it, South Island in Turkana. I may live to be a hundred or I may die any day. To my last moment I will carry with me the memory of those enchanted days and nights in Turkana with Aidan and Sveva. There was talk of war in the world during those days, tension growing in the Middle East, Iraqi threats, the invasion of Kuwait. The world was waiting ready to start a bloodshed born of mad pride and greed. It did not matter in Turkana.

We discovered a large twisted acacia on the side of the hill, growing alone and wise, barely out of the reach of the winds. And in turns we carried down to it what we had brought: mattresses and mats, jerrycans of drinking water, a cool-box full of food and a basket with the birthday cake – a chocolate heart that Sveva's *ayah*, Wanjiru, had packed lovingly, and to which Simon had added ten blue candles, and a handful of pink bougainvilleas, for *maridadi*, for beauty.

We set our belongings below the thorn tree, closely observed all the time by a couple of fantail ravens, whose territory we were clearly invading. Yet they did not seem to mind, and in fact eyed our food with eager fixity and undisguised anticipation. It was clear that they would become our constant companions, and to captivate them from the beginning, and show them we did not mind, I threw them some bread. Unwanted ravens and crows, I knew from experience, could become persistent pests, creeping about and spying for any chance to land and steal morsels of unguarded food.

We went for a swim in the warm soda water, down the sands of grey lava which held the sun's warmth long after it had set, walking into the lake awkwardly on slimy stones, always looking out for crocodiles. From the top of a rock we watched a large Nile perch darting around in her underwater territory. We rested on the hot sand and found crystals hidden in it like lost jewels.

At night we lit a fire of twigs which sparkled in distracted bursts with the wind blasts. We sat, with our back to a fallen branch of the acacia that was large enough to create a special protected corner for the three of us, cosy with pillows and straw mats. We opened a bottle of champagne and ate cold pasta; and, while a leg of lamb skewered with rosemary and wrapped in foil roasted on the fire, we told each other stories of the past.

Finally, with difficulty, we managed to light the ten large blue candles. The wax fizzed, melting quickly in the great heat. Sveva blew them out faster than the wind, and we all kissed each other, while our friends the ravens sang their raucous approval, guarding with tilted heads our celebration from the tallest branch.

No other little girl, we knew, was spending her birthday in such an improbable way, with only the wind and a lake for company. And the gods were smiling.

We spent two nights under that old acacia and shared the same blanket. Aidan climbed the parched hills looking for rare plants. We found bleached fish bones and brought them back to Simon, whose ancestors once used to live in Turkana.

Someone recently told me that they went to South Island and found some blue wax stuck to a branch of a solitary acacia tree. They could not work out what it was.

Eventually the house was reopened and inhabited again, new tenants lent it their fresh auras, and the shadows receded. Tonight the place was animated, garlands of coloured lights were strung from palm to palm to fight the black of the night. Music drifted high with the sea-breeze. The air, balmy with nocturnal jasmine, carried the voices of the festive crowd, and everyone was merry.

There were people I had not seen for years, the Kilifi crowd who used to come to our parties, the men who used to speak with Paolo of fishing, and even Mohammed, the retired old barman of the Mnarani Club, who for two generations had reigned behind his counter, knew all our children by name and, despite being a Muslim, remembered everyone's favourite drink. They were the times of the Lady Delamere Cup, when the boats assembled at sunrise to depart for the high seas, following a dream of marlin or sailfish, shark or tuna – or, at least, a great barracuda – and came back at late noon with red, blue and yellow flags flying in the wind, which we all tried to interpret through our binoculars to see who had caught most.

Then, Pimm's after wave of Pimm's, came the weighing and the marking on the old school blackboard. The winners were handed out prizes by a regal and cool Diana Delamere. Everyone clapped and talked about it for weeks. They had been other days, now gone forever, I could well see that. Then Diana had died, and an era with her.

The Mnarani had been sold to the tourist industry, and the old charm of days gone had vanished in the anonymous crowd which changed weekly. Paolo had died and, a few years after, Emanuele too. Charlie, the companion of Emanuele's school days, had been at the time still at military school in England. Soon afterwards, like his father before him, he had joined the Royal Navy. He had kept in touch, and when he was in Nairobi his tall lanky figure never failed to appear on our doorstep. I cared for him.

Dressed now in immaculate light white linen, his trim waist circled by a bottle-green cummerbund embroidered with a golden dragon, Charlie sat me at his right side, like the mother he had lost, and, like the son I had lost, I doted on him. His brown eyes, gentle twinkling eyes, brimmed with tears of remembrance and happy days.

'Remember when you told us about the baobab which moved in the full moon, and we believed you?'

'Remember when we celebrated Iain's birthday at the end of Ramadan down at the Mnarani, and Oria asked all the village women to cook ceremonial food and to lend their *buibuis*?'

'Remember when we found that gigantic puff-adder across the track below the Fielden house, blocking the way, and Emanuele refused to drive over it because we would have killed it, and we had to wait until he had coaxed it to move away slowly?'

'Remember when you gave a surprise party for Paolo's birthday and mine in the cove in the Kilifi Plantations? You had the cove lit with hundreds of candles, and you marked the line of the high tide with rows of lanterns, and you invited all Kilifi, and they all came!'

The magic cove. How could I ever forget? I fixed my eyes on the champagne glass I was holding, and through its golden bubbles, as in a yellow crystal ball, the memories swept back, of happy days.

When the ocean was green, with white rims to its waves, and the trade winds blew in Kilifi, Emanuele went sailing with his friend Charlie. I watched from the shore for their frail craft to pass, sitting under a giant baobab tree in our garden. This was a vast tree with a grey trunk spun with silver which seemed to absorb the heat of the sun like a human body, and it was my favourite refuge at the coast in the long afternoons.

They lifted their arms when they saw me, and the slimness of their young figures was emphasized by the swollen sail and the immensity of the ocean. Their boat cut away fast, bobbing on the waves in white sprays of foam, and disappeared behind the coral cliffs, leaving only an empty reef, and the colour of my wonder.

'I have discovered a fantastic place, Pep,' Emanuele told me one afternoon on his return, while still drying his damp blond fringe off his forehead. A glint of enthusiasm lit his dark eyes. 'A small cove, off the Kilifi Plantations. Charlie and I think you must come and see it. It would be great for a party.'

Next afternoon, we drove there together. It was not easy to find it from the jagged shore, as the terrain was covered with spiky sisal, taller than a man, and tangles of grassy twine. We located it finally, at the end of an inconspicuous trail. The boys helped me to climb down to it through rough old coral rocks hung with sea grapes, and we were there.

It was a semicircular cove of perfect proportions, surrounded by rugged grottoes at many levels, where one could instantly imagine hiding bright candles.

The tide was coming back, beating the shore of untarnished white sand, and decorating it with rows of seaweeds and coconut shells in lacy patterns. Seagulls flew low, with still wings and high calls piercing the evening. There was a rare, ageless purity about that place which enchanted me, and I could see that it would indeed be ideal for a special celebration.

It was the beginning of December 1979. Charlie's birthday had just been, Emanuele's would be in January, but Paolo's birthday was due in ten days or so, just before Christmas. There and then, we decided to give him a surprise party in the magic cove.

There began days of excitement and secret preparation. I

drove to the bazaars at the market in Mombasa, and bought mats of woven palm leaves to scatter on the sand, and bright cotton *kangas* and kapok to be sown into large cushions. From the workshop of the Kilifi Plantations, through which we had access to the cove, we borrowed steel drums and wire mesh for the barbecues, long low tables of driftwood, and planks of sawn timber to use as an improvised ladder to get down to the beach.

Early in the morning, when Paolo was out fishing, or in the late afternoons, we sneaked away to prepare the feast, to which we had invited, sworn to secrecy, everybody in Kilifi. We cleared the beach of debris deposited by generations of waves, swept the rocks of dried weeds and sand and finally started bringing down the assorted paraphernalia that we needed.

Then the day came, and I told Paolo that we had been asked to a special party on the beach. Puzzled and curious, he accepted happily.

We had worked since early morning carrying and decorating. Now the place was transformed, bright with candles, twinkling from the shelves of stones as in a fairy land. Paper lanterns marked the line of the high tide, and mats, covered in cushions of bright blues and turquoise, were strewn on the damp sand in a large circle round a roaring fire. Hurricane lamps and bunches of frangipani hung from stumps of driftwood. A music played with the sound of the wind.

A vast barbecue glowed in the largest cave, where meats were being roasted by my cook Gathimu. Large platters of pizzas and samosas, oysters and kebabs, garlic breads and cheeses, mangoes, papaya and pineapple were set out on a long table covered in banana leaves. Wine and champagne bottles stood in a wooden basin filled with ice, and a spicy punch of rum was served in half coconuts garnished with red hibiscus from a bowl with floating flowers. Up above,